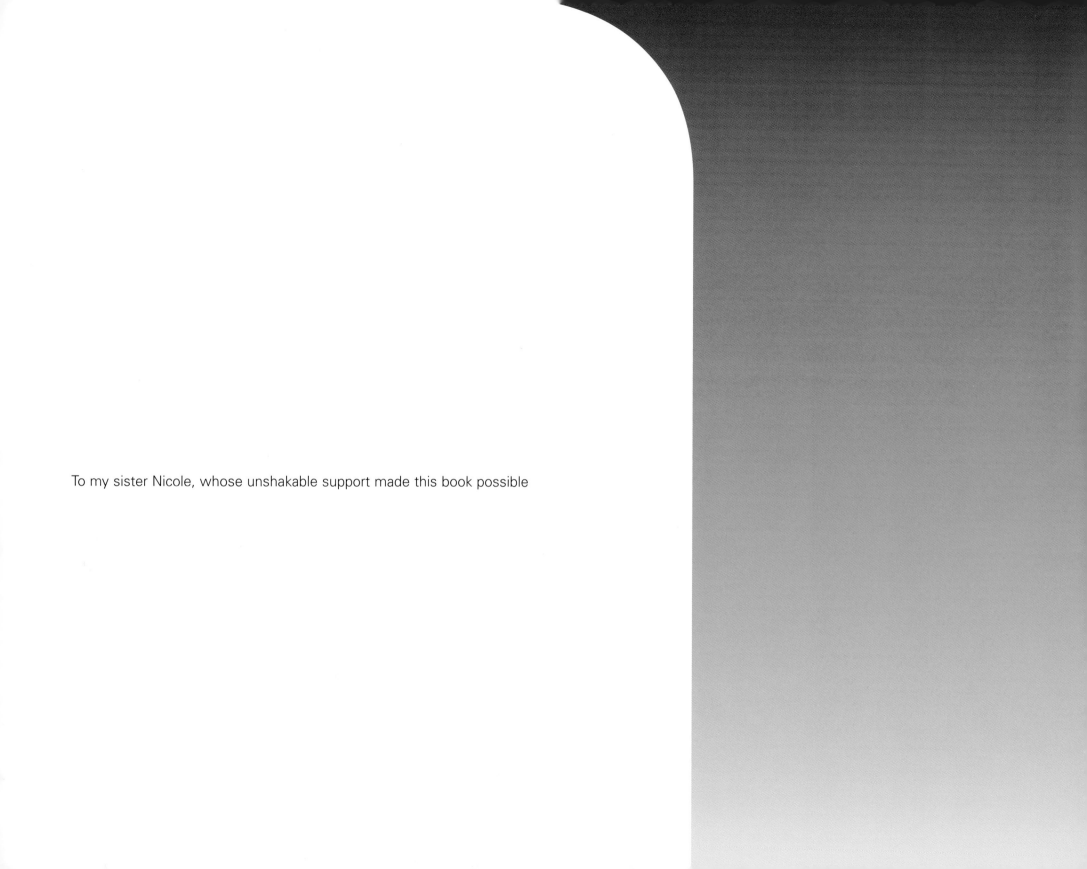

To my sister Nicole, whose unshakable support made this book possible

James Dean

From Passion for Speed to Immortality

James Dean
From Passion for Speed to Immortality

James Dean

From Passion for Speed to Immortality

Philippe Defechereux

First published 2005

ISBN Casebound: 1-85443-215-X

Printed and bound in Singapore by Star Standard

for the publisher

Dalton Watson Fine Books
1 Arundel Court, Elverlands Close,
Ferring, West Sussex BN12 5QE,
England

1730 Christopher Drive,
Deerfield, IL 60015,
USA

www.daltonwatson.com

Illustration on page 5: Early afternoon, September 30, 1955. James Dean happily fills his new Porsche, outside Los Angeles, headed north for what would have been his fourth race. He tragically died less than four hours later.

Contents

Prologue

The first time I picked up a biography of James Dean was in 1993 while on vacation in Arizona. I wanted to learn more about this great American legend as part of an endless quest to better understand my adopted country. The book was Joe Hyams' just published and brilliant *James Dean, Little Boy Lost*. Hyams is a Hollywood journalist who had known Jimmy and his circle quite intimately. The tale of James Dean instantly fascinated me and I felt a lot of kinship, being a bit of a rebel myself. Jimmy also loved cars and racing, a major hobby of mine. He even built scale models, as the photo opposite shows, as I still do. I read the book cover to cover in three days.

That's when the oddity struck me. Joe Hyams is so precise and accurate in his depiction of the Hollywood scene and of all the characters who were part of Jimmy's life; his quotes and locale descriptions were so detailed, I was terribly impressed until I got to the racing sections. As great a journalist as Joe Hyams is, I could quickly tell he knew little about European sports cars and even less about the California racing scene of the mid-1950s. Coincidentally, that was a topic I was researching at the time. I bought and read the other 23 biographies written about James Dean, and drew the same conclusion.

Then I looked at the calendar. In two years, 1995, it would be the 40th anniversary of Jimmy's death. I decided to research the subject in depth and write a long magazine piece about it. It turned into a small book which showed that Jimmy's zest for racing was an integral part of his character, his life, and his emotional quest to test himself and be the best at everything he did. Acting, racing and living were all part of the same script.

This year is the 50th anniversary of Jimmy's rise to fame and tragic death. He is still as well known worldwide as he was 50 years ago. Early last year, looking at this watershed anniversary, I decided to give a new look at my original work and turn it into a self-standing story, fully documented, incorporating new facts and more details about his life and acting career; showing even more clearly how Jimmy's racing ambitions were such a major part of his psyche, and what a critical role they played in his life and tragic death. The cars he owned and raced are also as beautiful to look at as the many famous Hollywood stars he was mingling with. Both are featured in the book. I hope you enjoy this extraordinary and dramatic story.

Philippe Defechereux

◀ James Dean, 'Jimmy', and cousin Markie in Fairmount building a scale model of a Jaguar XK120. This was during Jimmy's last visit to his home town in February, 1955 and shows another aspect of his passion for racing cars.

◀ James Dean at his
first official race in
Palm Springs in early
March 1955.

James Dean and his Racing Times
Michael T. Lynch

James Dean was one of the earliest and easily the most famous of an American archetype, the young rebel. He became a swaggering cultural icon whose cinematic image swept the world in the mid-1950s. He epitomized forever the dictum to live fast, die young and have a good-looking corpse. Over 25 books have been written about his life, yet none has properly explored his passion for fast cars and motorcycles, his skill on the racetrack and how his image is inextricably linked to speed and the cars he drove, both on and off the screen.

Most people think James Dean first arrived in California early in 1954, with his Warner Brothers contract and *Rebel Without a Cause* production just down the road. In fact, Dean had lived in Los Angeles from age 4 to 9, until his mother's death, when he went to live with relatives in Indiana. He returned to the City of Angels by interstate bus in 1949 after graduating from high school. Now a young adult, he had an intense interest in high-performance cars and motorcycles.

It was a heady time in Southern California. Los Angeles had prospered from its aircraft industry during World War II and the Cold War continued the demand for the latest aerospace products. Real estate development to sate the growing population was also creating fortunes. The area was awash in cash to pursue the residents' postwar craving for speed.

There was also change in the air in another major industry. The great screen stars of the thirties and forties were being challenged by a new generation of young actors.

◄ An early sports car event at Goleta, near Santa Barbara in 1949. Two pre-war French Talbots and an American Special lead the field toward the starting line for a time trial.

A typical Western field takes the start at Reno in October 1951. Bill Pollack's black Allard and Phil Hill's Jaguar share the front row while the bulk of the field is made up of modified MGs and Jaguars with some American Specials filling in. ▶

Most came from successes on Broadway like Marlon Brando, Montgomery Clift and Paul Newman. What they all had in common was their portrayal of alienated young men on the fringes of society, roles that would have been frowned upon during the studio system of earlier years. This was a theme that would also lift James Dean's career to the highest level of critical and public recognition.

The palm-lined boulevards of Southern California presented a vastly different streetscape from Dean's native Indiana. English motorcycles like Triumphs, BSAs and Velocettes challenged the pre-war dominance of American Harley-Davidsons and Indians on the roads and the racetracks. The situation with cars was the same. Hot Rods were plentiful, but what caught the eye of young car enthusiasts, from the Magic Mile of Wilshire Boulevard to the Pacific Coast Highway, were the MGs, Singers, Jaguars and other imports that were arriving at San Pedro harbor by the boatload. Dean had read about these dream machines in magazines, but seeing them in the metal engendered even more passion for them.

▲ A very young James Dean, his father Winton,
and the family's Chevrolet Master Series, in
Fairmount, Indiana, circa 1933.

After a sojourn in New York doing TV and stage work, Dean returned to California triumphantly in March 1954, to begin work on *Rebel Without a Cause*. He could now afford to go racing. The Southern California sports car racing scene that he plunged into was just entering its sixth season. After World War I, American racing had diverged from the European model of racing on public roads and courses that resembled them. With few exceptions, top line racing in the U.S. in the twenties and thirties was on oval tracks. A small group of preppies from the Northeast had tried with modest success, to revive European-style road racing before World War II through the Automobile Racing Club of America, but their efforts ended with Pearl Harbor.

As sports cars began to be imported after World War II, the Sports Car Club of America, founded in Boston in 1944, had a portion of its membership who wanted to race. They ultimately got their wish at Watkins Glen, New York on October 2, 1948. Although few realized it at the time, an American road racing revival was underway.

Southern California had almost been the site for the first post-war road race, when an event was scheduled at La Quinta, near Palm Springs, in February 1948. Like Watkins Glen, the idea was to attract tourists to the area. The organizer was Tommy Lee, a wealthy Cadillac distributor and owner of a radio network. Unfortunately, Lee was involved in an automobile accident before the event, the town fathers lost their nerve and the race was cancelled.

After the successful Watkins Glen race, other events were held in the East in 1949, but Southern Californians continued to cast about for a suitable venue. A group in Northern California held a race at Buchanan Field in suburban San Francisco in November 1949. Southern California finally joined the trend in April 1950, when the California Sports Car Club staged a race at Palm Springs.

Sports car racing continued to grow throughout the country and the Sports Car Club of America (SCCA) initiated National Championships in several classes of production (stock) and modified (cars built primarily for racing) cars. By 1953, the SCCA arranged to race on courses situated on Strategic Air Command (SAC) air bases . The SAC was responsible for the long-range bombers that would attack Russia in the event of war and was a powerful political force. The head of the SAC was General Curtis LeMay, a sports car enthusiast who later became Secretary of Defense in the Kennedy administration. With the SAC's publicity machine behind the races, tremendous exposure was achieved for the new sport and by the mid-1950s, single races often attracted 100,000 people. This put some sports car races on attendance parity with the Indianapolis 500, then by far, America's most publicized race.

In California, the Northern part of the state was loyal to the Sports Car Club of America, which sanctioned events there. Like many private clubs of the day, the SCCA sometimes tended toward racism and anti-Semitism in their membership policies. Southern California was less formal and races there were sanctioned by the California Sports Car Club. Even then, the Los Angeles basin had a much more diverse population than the San Francisco Bay area, and the Cal Club membership reflected this. There was a healthy rivalry between drivers from the two parts of the state and a driver racing outside his region would often find himself assigned a starting position deep in the field.

After its slow start, California had reached parity with the Northeast by 1955, when James Dean came on the racing scene. Western venues like Torrey Pines, Palm Springs and Pebble Beach now had traditions almost as long as Watkins Glen and Bridgehampton in the East. The starting grids in California had evolved from ragged groups of MGs, pre-war cars, hot rods adapted to road racing and mangy backyard specials. By 1955, California drivers were winning the two big production classes with Mercedes 300 SLs and Porsches. The overall race winners were now exotic, glamorous Ferraris and Maseratis, not far removed from factory team specification.

When Dean decided to go racing, he was part of a long Hollywood involvement in the sport. Actor Jackie Cooper raced and Keenan Wynn was a car owner. Clark Gable and Gary Cooper often acted as track officials and many other Hollywood stars, including James Stewart, took part in trophy presentations at races.

Road races at that time had four major classes, under and over 1500 cubic centimeters of engine size in the production and modified classes. Porsche Super Speedsters had recently come to the U.S. market and they offered the most potential in the under-1500 cc production class. They were in short supply, with long waiting lists, but Porsche dealer, John von Neumann sold one to Dean, almost certainly putting him ahead of other orders.

Dean faced formidable odds in his quest for victory. Part of becoming a successful driver is to acquire as much track time as possible. Because of the weather in Southern California, racing went on year round. The Eastern season was interrupted by snow, while even Northern California suffered winter rains. Thus, Southern Californian drivers could rack up more racing mileage in a season than those from other parts of the country could in several.

That track time was converting into victories for drivers against whom Dean had to compete. Despite the fact that most points-paying races in the SCCA National Championships were held east of the Rocky Mountains, five of the fourteen National Champions in class were from the West Coast in 1955, Dean's year on the tracks. Drivers like Phil Hill, Dan Gurney and Richie Ginther were winning the races that Dean attended as a spectator and racer. These were Dean's heroes and represented the kind of competition that he had to face. Their California-bred careers would lead all three to the

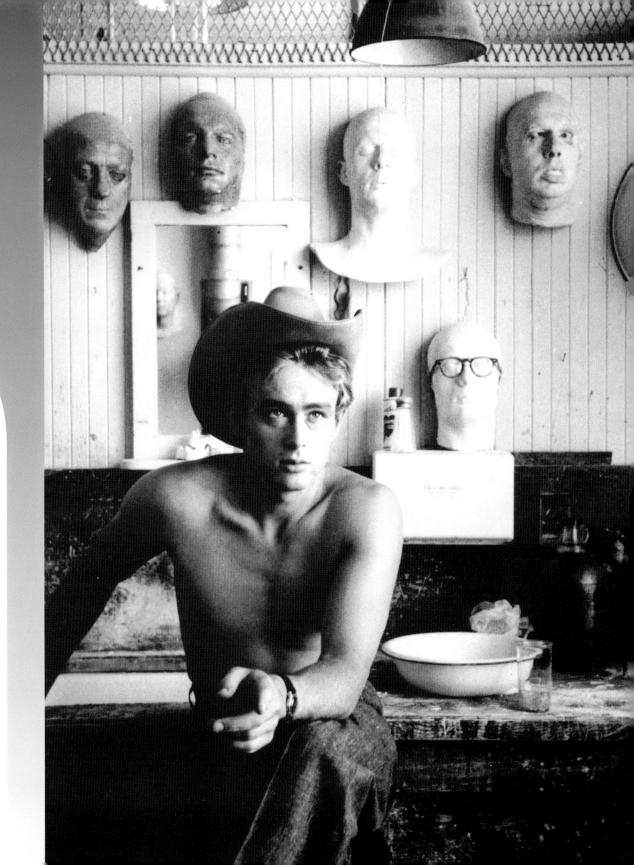

◀ A splendid illustration of Jimmy's passion for race cars. Here, he lovingly washes his Porsche 356 Super Speedster in March. 1955.

Influenced by his mother, Jimmy developed many artistic talents besides acting. He took classes in music, sculpture, dancing and photography. This photo shows him in a sculptor's studio. ▶

pinnacle of road racing, factory drives on Grand Prix teams in Europe like Ferrari, BRM and Porsche. Hill would go on to win the World Grand Prix Championship for Ferrari in 1961.

In Dean's first four races against this kind of talent, he won his class three times and finished second once. This was an outstanding accomplishment for an amateur with no previous organized racing experience. Dean's reputation as a reckless, wild man behind the wheel is grossly uninformed. *James Dean: From Passion for Speed to Immortality* presents facts, not hype, about Dean's racing career and his fatal accident. These facts have been drawn from painstaking research ranging from period quotes, police reports, witness statements and other documents of the time. Much of this information has not been available to the public in the past. The book adds to our knowledge of James Dean's life and assures that his racing career will be more widely understood and not simply a footnote to the colorful history of Southern California road racing in the 1950s.

Chapter One

Friday
September 30
1955

◀ Pages 18-19: James Dean zooming northward towards Salinas, near Monterey, on his way to his fourth race. Seated next to him is Rolf Wütherich, his dedicated German mechanic. This is the last photo of James Dean alive.

◀ In this scene from *East of Eden*, the two brothers, rebellious Cal (James Dean) and conventional Aron (Dick Davalos) try to make up, while Aron's girlfriend, Abra (Julie Harris) looks on dubiously.

▶ James Dean as Cal and Raymond Massey as Adam in a famous scene from *East of Eden* where father and son are fighting.

As a radiant sun slowly dipped towards the Pacific Ocean, its reddening glow accented a wide grin on Jimmy Dean's intense, boyish face. Tightly seated into the cockpit of his 'baby', a brand new silver Porsche 550 Spyder, Jimmy was speeding north towards the San Joaquin Valley, Hollywood rapidly receding behind him. The September air was gentle, warm and inviting. The streamlined little racer sliced through it smoothly, humming in fourth gear with obvious contentment.

Now Jimmy shifted gears to tackle the grades of the Tejon Pass, about 30 miles south of Bakersfield. The addictive pangs triggered by speed tugged once more inside his gut. He pushed his slippery Porsche a bit harder, increasing the rush he always felt when revving wheeled machines close to their limit.

Though he had been seeking the wondrous halo of acting stardom for a long time, the limelight of Hollywood, reached just months before this trip north to Salinas, was still new and awkward for him. In contrast, he had been at ease with fast bikes and souped-up cars since his early teenage years. He had tested himself endlessly with these on every possible stretch of road whenever he had a chance. Today still only twenty-four, if Jimmy felt he had mastery over anything, it was over fast machinery.

Suddenly, the Porsche crested the eastern peak of the San Rafael Mountains and the vast Central Valley came into view. Jimmy would now drive on northward to Salinas, some 20 miles east of Monterey, a further four hours or so of driving time. There, over the coming weekend, he would compete in the fourth sports car event of his budding career as a racecar driver, piloting the 550 Spyder, a new Porsche model built for sheer performance and produced in very limited numbers for racing pros or serious amateurs.

On the track, with this potent racing car, Jimmy would experience his favorite thrill: controlling a sleek, torquey sportster subjected to vast opposing forces,

teasing the limits of the laws of nature, defying fate; struggling at once against his own fears and the courage of other spirited men. In this arena he felt sure he would triumph over the odds, as he had in acting, and experience pure joy. "It's the only time I feel whole", he had said of racing.

A mere two weeks earlier, Jimmy had completed his role in the movie *Giant* alongside co-stars Elizabeth Taylor, Rock Hudson and Carroll Baker. That was his third major feature film, all three wrapped in just the last eighteen months.

East of Eden was his first and had been released nationwide in March, only six months previously. The movie was based on John Steinbeck's novel of the same title. A modern allegory of the contest between Cain and Abel for their father's love and devotion, it had been set in the lush Salinas valley, representing Eden.

The main protagonists were the puritanical father, not so subtly called Adam Trask, and his two sons, Cal (Cain) and Aron (Abel). Jimmy's riveting interpretation of Cal Trask, the rebellious one, rejected and needy, impulsive but deserving, had catapulted him instantly into early stardom, quickly drawing large crowds of adoring teenagers across the country.

The first post-war generation connected spontaneously with the young actor's potent rendition of its brewing rebellion against the adult world of 1950's America. For the first time, someone their age was breaching the pervasive but worn-out pretense of the ideal family; someone was acting out in a mass medium their deep sense of alienation from the adult world. Jimmy's second film, aptly titled *Rebel Without A Cause*, had a similar theme and would open across the country in just another four days. Based on early reviews, it showed even more promise for popular success.

So now, less than two years since he had left New York, as he drove on northward in his growling Spyder, Jimmy had satisfied his prodigious challenge to reach Hollywood stardom. But rest on his fresh laurels he could not. Another burning passion needed to be consumed. His other, seemingly impossible childhood dream, also must be fulfilled. He was on his way, he thought, to achieving it.

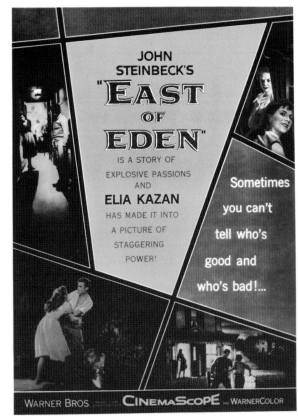

▲ A Warner Brothers poster for *East of Eden*, the movie that put the name James Dean on the map. It was released in March, 1955.

◄ James Dean and Elizabeth Taylor 'horsing around' on the set of *Giant* in Marfa, Texas. Jimmy, the junior star, instantly rose to the level of the already acclaimed actress.

◄ James Dean as Cal in *East of Eden*, looking at the beanfield from which he hopes to raise money for his father. Though a financial success, the venture will lead to a bitter break with his father.

Chapter Two

Early Days
and Influences

Early Days and Influences

◀ Pages 24-25: Jimmy returned to Fairmount for what would be the last time in February, 1955. In the background is the farm of his uncle, Marcus Winslow, where he was raised.

▲ A young Jimmy tries a first set of wheels in California, before his mother's tragic death returned him to Indiana at age 9.

Jimmy, though near-sighted, was also an accomplished athlete. He played in his High School's basketball team and, as shown here, baseball team. Jimmy is in the middle of the front row. ▶

James Byron Dean was born near the farming town of Fairmount, Indiana, on February 8, 1931. His mother, Mildred was interested in art and literature. She often read poetry to her young son, and at one point even built a cardboard stage where they would invent plays together. Jimmy was thus attracted to acting and theater from an early age. His father, Winton Dean, a dental technician, was more aloof, though still a loving man.

In 1935, when Jimmy was only four, Winton was offered a more remunerative job in Santa Monica, California, and the young family moved west to the Pacific Coast. At first, the new surroundings appeared ideal, but tragedy soon struck. In the early part of 1940, when Jimmy was just nine, Mildred, though only twenty-nine years old, was diagnosed with advanced breast cancer.

Despite intensive treatment, she died that year on July 14th, leaving a gaping wound in her son's psyche that would never heal.

A train took Mildred's body back to Indiana to be buried near where she had been born; a mourning Winton and his devastated son accompanying the coffin. After the funeral, following a family meeting, it was agreed that Jimmy would be better off staying in

Fairmount, to be raised by Ortense, Mildred's sister, and her husband Marcus Winslow. Winton, deep in debt due to the heavy medical expenses incurred attempting to save his wife's life, would return to Santa Monica and resume his practice there.

Jimmy, it is clear, was transformed by the tragic experience. Following his beloved mother's lead, and as if to take revenge upon fate, he set out to become a star in the performing arts. At Fairmount High, he took every opportunity he was given to take acting classes and appear on stage. Tutored by Adeline Nall, a renowned drama and speech teacher, he made rapid progress, and his perseverance paid off. He won his first major award in 1949, at age eighteen, which earned him a feature article with his picture on the front page of the *Fairmount News*.

During those same years, Jimmy had developed an equally intense passion for wheeled machines. He was given his first motorized bike, an American-made Whizzer when he was fourteen. A gift from his Uncle Marcus, the comparatively tame contraption turned the youth into a speed junkie almost instantly. Then a bespectacled teenager, Jimmy would push the Whizzer at night on the most demanding dirt roads he could find, always testing his own limits. Endowed with exceptional driving skills, he quickly outgrew the capabilities of the simple motorbike.

▲ Jimmy in Fairmount on his beloved Czech motorbike, a gift from his uncle Marcus Winslow. It was not his first motorbike, and would not be his last.

◄ Jimmy in his High School graduation garb in Fairmount, Indiana. Soon after, he would move back to California and live with his father, taking acting classes at UCLA.

▸ A famous shot of Jimmy on a street in New York in 1954. Though looking dapper here, his life in New York was harsh as he had very little money while he was trying desperately to advance his acting career.

A few months later, Uncle Marcus presented him with a new Czech, a full-bore motorcycle imported from Czechoslovakia. Marcus had bought it at Marvin Carter's shop in Fairmount, where Jimmy eventually spent endless hours talking gears, learning to tweak engines and how to tease maximum performance from them without excessive strain. He loved riding his motorcycle, and soon could perform frightening stunts, like lying flat on the saddle at a top speed of almost 50 miles per hour. Uncle Marcus remarked later: "he never got hurt, and he never found anything he couldn't do well almost the first time he tried it. Just one fall off the bike and he would have been afraid of speed, but he was without fear".

Cars came next. Along with several schoolmates, Jimmy first drove a friend's souped-up '34 Plymouth. On those weekends, the band would test its members on a dirt road on the outskirts of town featuring a tight S twist which boys called 'Suicide Curve'. In no time, Jimmy became the only one who dared go through the curve at top speed, while still maintaining full control of the Plymouth. The single kid who came closest to him rolled the car over. Such feats soon earned him the nickname 'One-Speed-Dean'. The only speed he knew, the people of Fairmount said, was flat out.

His first regular car was Uncle Marcus' new 1949 Ford Custom. Jimmy drove it to school almost every day, and used it to go to his high school senior prom in 1949. Little did he know how much Ford Customs

◀ Jimmy and Geraldine Page in a New York
restaurant in 1954. They were together in
the play *The Immoralist* and Jimmy no doubt
is trying to learn as much as he can from
his more experienced colleague.

▼ Jimmy playing the bongo drums.
These were his favorite instruments and
he liked to enjoy their rhythmic sound
everywhere he went.

would affect the rest of his life at every major turn.

Later that summer Jimmy made a bold move,
traveling by bus to California to rejoin his then-remarried
father and take serious acting classes, hopefully at
UCLA. Though Winton proved patient, he was against
Jimmy aiming for an acting career, preferring him to
go to Santa Monica City College and study to become
an accountant or a lawyer. But the reason Jimmy
had moved to Los Angeles was to further his acting
career, as there were no schools in Indiana offering
such an opportunity.

The father-son relationship remained quietly tense,
though Winton bought Jimmy a '39 Chevy to assuage
him. Jimmy did enlist in Santa Monica City College as a
Physical Education major, but by the summer of 1950,

he left his father's house, enrolled in UCLA's theatre arts
program and moved into the Sigma Nu fraternity house.
For two years, he did everything imaginable in order to
break through as an actor. "Some men bet on horses,
or dogs, I gamble on myself," he explained. He only
landed a minor role in a Pepsi Cola commercial and a
few other commercial spots.

In the fall of 1951, he made a significant change,
moving to New York where Broadway plays were
considered an ideal launching pad for a Hollywood
career. There, he soon found acting roles in a few minor
television series, and a friend who lent him a fast
Norton motorcycle. In no time, he had frightened many
co-riding dates and pals, zooming fearlessly through the
tight, crowded street grid of Manhattan.

◀ Jimmy in Fairmount in February, 1955.
He is visiting the grave of his grandfather,
Cal Dean, with little cousin Markie, son of
Marcus Winslow. The remarkable coincidence
is that in *East of Eden*, the character played
by Jimmy was also named Cal.

Though Jimmy experienced only six months
of celebrity before he died, several famous
photographers of the day were assigned to
record his life and antics. Here, Sandy Roth,
photographer on assignment for *Collier's*
magazine, takes a double profile of mask
and actor. ▶

Eventually, Jimmy's growing talent resulted in
Broadway roles. He was cast next to two major stars,
Geraldine Page and Louis Jourdan, in an adaptation of
André Gide's *The Immoralist*. That is how, in February
of 1954, he caught the attention of Elia Kazan, the up-
and-coming director with successes such as *On The
Waterfront*, starring Marlon Brando, already under his
belt. Brando, seven years Jimmy's senior and
Hollywood's hottest male star with movie hits like
A Street Car Named Desire and *Viva Zapata!* to his
credit, was very much his role model. When casting for
East of Eden, Kazan set up a competitive session in
New York. Jimmy eventually was chosen over another
upcoming star, Paul Newman; while Julie Harris
prevailed over Joanne Woodward for the lead female
role – as Aron's girlfriend who eventually turned to Cal.
On April 7, 1954, Jimmy found himself in Hollywood
holding a signed contract with Warner Brothers.

Chapter Three

Hollywood Beginnings
From Bikes to Racers

◀ Pages 32-33: Man and machine as one. One can almost sense mutual love from this glorious shot by Sandy Roth.

▲ Marlon Brando in an archetypal scene of *The Wild Ones*, a movie that in a certain way prefigured *Rebel*. Brando was Jimmy's first big role model.

◀ Jimmy and his powerful motorcycle shortly after his arrival in Hollywood under contract from Warner Brothers. He is brimming with happiness.

Jimmy's infatuation with instruments of speed only intensified after his breakthrough move to Hollywood. He spent his first movie actor's wages on a second-hand, British-made Triumph motorbike, a choice that was no accident. Brando's latest success in 1954 was *The Wild Ones*, a film in which he played the leader of a 'bad' motorcycle gang challenging the establishment. "Nobody tells me what to do" was one of his defining lines in the movie, in which the badge of Brando's Triumph motorbike was highly visible. This was an early example of deliberate 'product placement' in a Hollywood production.

As soon as he could afford it, Jimmy exchanged the 5T for the most powerful Triumph model, the T-110. As he had done in New York, every time he could persuade a friend or date to ride with him, the young maverick relished terrifying the hapless soul in daredevil swoops up and down the twisty canyon roads of Tinsel Town. Later in May of that year, shortly before production began on *East of Eden*, Jimmy took his first step to owning a racy car: he bought a red MG TD, a sportster; souped-up but nonetheless quite affordable.

MGs had been all the rage for beginners in American road races since 1948. After taking the two-seater for its

first spin, Jimmy translated his exhilaration in a revealing letter to girlfriend Barbara Glenn in New York: "A new addition has been added to the Dean family. I got a red '53, MG (milled head etc. hot engine). My sex pours itself into fast curves, broadslides and broodings; drags, etc. You have plenty of competition now. My motorcycle, my MG and my girl. I have been sleeping with my MG We make it together. HONEY".

The small, featherweight British sportster was one of the early exciting European cars to gain favor with sizable groups of American drivers. In those days, Detroit simply did not build racing or even sports cars, leaving Europe as the only reliable supplier of driving fun. American automobile executives were content with making cars that just *looked* good. Their next priority was cuddly comfort. As a result, in the mid-Fifties, the pioneering technologies that busied Detroit's research departments were automatic transmissions, air conditioning and large engines with lots of power designed for affordability and ease of maintenance, but not performance. A safer chassis, better brakes and more capable suspension designs were abysmally low on their priority list, as was any interest in racing.

The choice for enthusiasts among domestic products was thus narrowly limited to a hodge-podge of homemade 'specials' or upgraded one-of-a-kind hot-rods, often based on 1930s production models. It is little wonder then that the growing number of Americans with a passion for driving or racing bought European machinery. The MG and newer but kindred sports cars such as Allards, Porsches, Ferraris and Jaguars quickly became the favorite ride of car-lovers and *aficionados* on both coasts of America. Racing drivers with such cars also quickly monopolized podiums on road racing circuits, just at a time when this form of the sport, highly popular in Europe since early in the century, was finally making major inroads in the New World.

MGs made up the largest part of the fields in early US postwar racing. This is John von Neumann at Torrey Pines in December 1951, where he retired. This car, with body modifications by Emil Diedt, was considered the fastest unsupercharged MG on the West Coast.

American Specials were odd combinations of various chassis and engines based on the imagination and loyalties of their owners or designers. This is Bill Eschrich and his Offenhauser Special, winner of the Sunday consolation race in Santa Barbara, where Jimmy blew a piston while in fourth place.

In 1955, the year James Dean raced, the Ferrari Monza was the car to have if you wanted to win the 'Main Event'. Its 3.0 liter engine had twice the displacement of the Porsche 550 motor. This is John von Neumann at Santa Barbara during Memorial Day weekend, where Jimmy raced his Porsche 356 for the third and last time.

To be competitive, sports cars had to have as light and rigid a chassis as possible, a smart suspension and strong brakes; the whole being pulled by a high-revving engine through a complex but sturdy gearbox. Road racing required a full set of superior skills from the driver. Spectators at road racing events were usually more thrilled by the display of driving techniques around corners than the spectacular pageantry of stadium racing. This version of the sport drew a very different crowd from the ovals, which had dominated the American racing scene since the early 1920s.

Oval tracks were little more than modified horse tracks, themselves direct descendents of the Roman circus. Ovals made it easy to stage pre-race spectacles - the high-school band parade - and control ticket sales at the gate, and therefore generate profits. But they required more brawn than skill from drivers, and little but raw power from the cars, similar to the chariots of Roman times. In order to have a chance to stand on the podium, oval racers needed to go very fast, handling only left turns, using reasonably smooth tracks, and never in the rain! In fact, most of the Specials that had raced at Indianapolis in May 1955 were little evolved from their ancestors of the 1930s, except for the engine and body shape. They still had solid axles and leaf-spring suspensions, a design dating back to the horse carriages of the eighteenth century.

For Jimmy, the choice had been easy. He prized driving skills acquired on challenging roads over raw speed and wanted a car built for that purpose. He would only own European sports cars. In early March, three weeks before *Rebel* was in production, he had exchanged his MG for a more potent racer. It was a Porsche 356 Super Speedster, a white factory-built ragtop model with a boosted engine displacing 1.5 liter (91.5 cubic inches). It delivered 70 horsepower and could reach just over 100 miles per hour. The Porsche appeared to be a big jump for him, but it was a machine with which he could win races.

35

The film script he was rehearsing at the time had possibly influenced his motivation for a faster car. *Rebel's* turning point was the 'Chickie Run' between the hot rods of two rival teenagers: loner Jim Stark (played by Jimmy) and gang leader Buzz Gunderson (Corey Allen). Daring each other for pride as well as Judy's heart (Natalie Wood), they would race two cars side by side towards a high cliff. The first one to bail out before the edge would be the 'chicken', losing face in front of his peers and Judy. Before climbing into his '46 Ford, Jim would put on his favorite red nylon windbreaker zippered in the front, while Buzz wore his usual black leather jacket.

As the gang and Judy looked on, the two cars, accelerating side by side, would roar towards the edge. Jim would jump out at the last possible instant, but Buzz's jacket sleeve became entangled in the door handle. Trapped in his metal cage, he would die after crashing on the rocky beach below. After grieving at the tragedy, Judy's heart soon would turn toward Jim. At the movie's end, Judy and Jim were lovers.

Of note in the early part of the script, Buzz drove his gang members in his personal car, a splendid 1952 Ford Custom convertible, a model akin to the car the young actor from Indiana had driven to his prom.

Jimmy had bought his first Porsche from John von Neumann, a racing driver himself and a well-known importer of European sports cars in California. The son of a famous Viennese surgeon, von Neumann was involved with cars almost as soon as he settled on the

West Coast before World War II. In late 1948, he had opened his own shop in North Hollywood and called it Competition Motors, leaving no doubts as to his interests. The round-faced Austrian started racing with a pre-war Jaguar SS100, and later on an extensively modified MG TD. He had switched to a German racer in 1952, a stubby Porsche 356 Coupe built in Gmünd, Austria, which was Dr. Porsche's first factory site. After three races in that new car, he judged its winning potential in California as excellent, despite its relatively heavy weight.

American sports car events were run on much shorter tracks than those in Europe, making sprinting speed more important than sturdy endurance. As a result, a light weight, agile car was a better choice to win in California races. To meet his ambitions, von Neumann proceeded to saw off the Porsche's roof, and then adjusted the chassis, suspension and brakes accordingly. In so doing, he turned his homemade roadster into a regular class winner, soon relegating MGs to also-rans. That success helped build traffic in the Competition Motors showroom, especially from the circles of young and wealthy movie stars.

The Model 356 was the first car to bear the name Porsche. Introduced in 1948 as an affordable sportster, the 356 was post-war Germany's first new design to reach the market, ahead of the Mercedes-Benz 300 series. It was a sporting two-seater designed for thrilling drives. Private customers quickly demonstrated its class-winning capabilities on a variety of circuits and daunting road courses. This boosted the new model's commercial success and firmly established Porsche as a carmaker. In 1954, these unusual-looking cars with an air-cooled engine located in the rear had found nearly six hundred new owners in the United States alone. That represented 40 percent of Porsche's total production of nine cars per day. Many of Porsche's American and European fans bought their 356s with racing in mind.

The moment Jimmy acquired his zippy Super Speedster, he immediately set to work to master it sufficiently in order to enter an official race. And so he began behaving in a way that his school mates from Fairmount would have instantly recognized. Turning Mulholland Drive into his own private test track, he set out for endless practice runs up and down its hills. The famous road is a twisty two-lane affair snaking and weaving along the crest of the Santa Monica Mountains for nearly 20 miles, connecting Laurel Canyon in Hollywood with Topanga Canyon in Woodland Hills.

Jimmy racked up nearly a thousand miles at hair-raising speeds in a little over a week. This allowed him to become intimately familiar with his car. It also raised concerns, though not among those who knew him well. Commented a friend: "Some people thought he would break his neck, but we didn't worry about him - one thing about Jimmy, he possessed an amazing set of reflexes and his coordination was perfect."

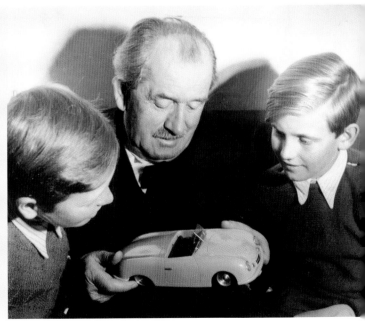

John von Neumann, the spectacularly ▲ successful Viennese emigré. He owned the Porsche-VW distributorship for Southern California and raced a wide range of great racing cars.

Dr. Ferdinand Porsche with his two grandsons and a scale model of a mid-engined Porsche Roadster, the first car to bear the name Porsche. The grandson on the right is Ferdinand Piëch, who would become chairman of VW-Audi in 1994 and turn the then-ailing company around. ▶

◀ Jimmy at the wheel of his new Porsche 356 Super Speedster in Hollywood. He might have been on his way to Mulholland Drive in order to hone his racing skills.

Hollywood Beginnings: From Bikes to Racers

During this time, Jimmy took Natalie Wood for a drive on the same road. After yet another wild sprint, he purposely parked in a spot offering the best scenic view of the lit metropolis lower in the valley. The next day, in a great deal of excitement, he called several friends, begging them to join him for lunch at the studio and claiming mysteriously: "It can be done." Lew Bracker, his insurance agent, and Joe Hyams, the journalist, accepted and met a beaming Jimmy in the restaurant. Bragging and grinning, he told them that he had just broken through yet another barrier: "We found a way to make love in the Speedster. We did the impossible."

Jimmy knew that Natalie Wood, then 16, was having simultaneous affairs with Nick Ray, the director of *Rebel*, and Dennis Hopper, another of the movie's teenage stars. This only added to his delight about the feat he had just performed. Despite the competition, he had won the girl over, aided by his car, just as in *Rebel*.

Nick Ray was a most interesting character and the brains behind *Rebel*. He was 43 years old when he began to work on *Rebel*, with many movies under his belt, such as *Knock on Any Door* with Humphrey Bogart, *In a Lonely Place* (also with Bogart) and *Johnny Guitar*, a great box office hit. He was on his second marriage in 1955, and would be on his fourth marriage when he died in 1979. He was a friend of Elia Kazan, the man who had 'discovered' James Dean for *East of Eden*. Nick Ray had an instant affinity for Jimmy and wanted him as the central character of *Rebel*. He successfully imposed Jimmy on Warner Brothers, brushing aside other upcoming stars, such as Robert Wagner and John Kerr.

When time came to select the rebellious girl who would fall in love with Jimmy, candidates abounded. Nick Ray looked at Julie Harris who stared in *East of Eden*, Joanne Woodward, even Jayne Mansfield and several others. When Natalie Wood, desperately wanting the role, was introduced to him, Nick Ray was instantly taken. In fact, rumor says that they became lovers in less than two weeks. She got the part and also proved she was correctly cast.

An early famous moment in *Rebel*: the knife fight between Jim Stark (James Dean) and Buzz Gunderson (Corey Allen), the gang leader. The outcome will lead to the 'Chickie Run' dare by Buzz. ▶

Another famous moment in *Rebel*. As the 'Chickie Run' is about to start, Judy (Natalie Wood), girlfriend of Jim Stark's (James Dean) rival Buzz Gunderson (Corey Allen), approaches Jim to give him encouragement. Minutes later, Buzz will have lost his dare and died, giving the plot an entirely new turn. ▼

James Dean and *Rebel* director Nicholas Ray. The two had strong professional affinities for each other, though the relationship was filled with tensions which Ray exploited to further the intensity of Jimmy's acting in the movie. It was a fabulous success.

◀ A beaming James Dean enjoying his budding celebrity on the set of *Giant* in Marfa, Texas. His riveting performances in *East of Eden* and *Rebel* helped launch the youth revolution, and the cult of teenage idols.

A striking photo of the defiant Jim (James Dean) and Judy (Natalie Wood) in *Rebel*. ▶

The script of *Rebel* was based on a 1944 clinical study of imprisoned, disturbed youth by Dr. Robert M. Lindner. Nick Ray's stroke of genius was to transform the original plot by switching the key characters from poor street punks to troubled middle-class teenagers with whom many of America's youth could identify. Jimmy's contemporaries all shared to a degree the emotional restlessness that stirred his soul, his addictive search for ever new forms of 'self-experience', his deep insecurities and core narcissism. These 'rebels', later dubbed the 'Beat Generation'

by the media, generated a powerful undertow below the wave of more traditional youth then rising eventually to engulf the entire country. They defiantly challenged the boredom, conformity and bourgeois hypocrisies of post-World War II society, breaking taboos in their own brazen ways throughout their community, questioning all aspects of American culture. At around the time Jimmy was practicing in his new Porsche, Bill Haley & His Comets were shaking up the music world, taking *Rock Around The Clock* all the way to the top of the hit parade. Elvis Presley had begun popularizing Black

Blues and Country Music in the South. Marlon Brando and Marilyn Monroe, flaunting their raw sensual appeal, were breaking other taboos. On university campuses, Jack Kerouac and Allen Ginsberg were unleashing their strange new literary genius, spawning what later would be called the underground culture. These were still very much fringe movements, but they would ripen rapidly and explode into a full-scale social revolution in the 1960s.

◄ Jimmy as Cal and Julie Harris as Abra in *East of Eden* at the moment when the rebellious son wins the heart of his brother's girlfriend.

Fairmount, February 1955. Jimmy giving cousin Markie a push in a home-built 'soap box' racer. ▶

When *East of Eden* opened in early March, Jimmy's first movie proved an instant hit. The rage, anger and fears expressed by him on the screen with such natural vehemence and talented intensity had spectators and critics alike enthralled. The word spread quickly to 'Bobby Soxers' and their male peers, who rushed to see the movie in large numbers. The fan mail started pouring in. Almost overnight, James Dean became a star among the youth audience and movie enthusiasts, though remaining mostly unknown to the majority of their parents. Still, Hollywood quickly sensed the awesome power he possessed. Warner Brothers, wishing to generate even more publicity for Jimmy's coming movies, now also mentioned his passion for fast cars and his racing ambitions. This was intended to reinforce his 'no-holds-barred' image, one of the keys to his early appeal.

Chapter Four

On to Official Racing

◀ Pages 44-45: Santa Barbara, Memorial Day weekend event, 1955. Jimmy at full speed in his Porsche 356. He would soon blow a piston and have to give up. This would turn out to be his last race.

▲ A typical driver briefing at Santa Barbara. The casualness and informality are plain to see. Although this was now a civilian airport, in the background, one spots the hangars where World War II US Marine fighter aircraft were sheltered between active crew training.

▶ Ken Miles racing his highly modified MG R-2, dubbed the 'Flying Shingle', at Santa Barbara's 1955 Memorial Day event which he won. Miles

went all the way up the racing hierarchy and won a seat in the official Ford International World Championship team. He died in a crash while testing a new Ford Le Mans prototype at Riverside, CA, in 1966.

Cy Yedor and his own highly modified MG R-1 racing at Santa Barbara's 1955 Memorial Day event. Like Jimmy, he was beaten by more powerful cars. ▶

Jimmy's amazing climb towards Hollywood fame was still a mere glimmer of hope when he had bought the Super Speedster. Keeping his budding movie career from his racing ambitions fully separate in his mind, he had purchased the Porsche on March 1, before the release of *East of Eden*, and shortly after hearing that the California Sports Car Club (CSCC) was organizing its eighth race weekend in Palm Springs later that month. Jimmy's first opportunity to test himself in a real-life 'Chickie Run' was at hand. He filed an entry within days, anticipating his first sanctioned event with a great deal of glee. To Warner Brother's consternation, he failed to attend a star-filled premiere of his first movie, staged as a prestigious gala benefit at the Astor theater in New York. The celebrity usherettes, Marlene Dietrich, Marilyn Monroe and Eva Marie Saint were left to provide the glamour without their expected male counterpart.

Racing was foremost on Jimmy's mind. And after so much dedicated practice on open roads, he was finally going to have a chance to prove his skills against experienced drivers on a real track, in full view of the press and public. As the weekend approached and *East of Eden* became an unexpectedly strong hit, the participation of Hollywood's new star in a real car race drew some serious attention. Only the tight community of experienced drivers remained unimpressed. Star status in their book required a much more manly set of talents and achievements than the ability to excite teenage movie viewers. Famous California driver Phil Hill, then a young talented driver who, in 1961, would become America's first Formula 1 champion, admits that Jimmy was not taken seriously at first. He recalls hearing Sam Weill, a von Neumann associate, utter "Here comes the Mickey Mouse Brando" upon seeing Jimmy enter the Competition Motors premises. Hill felt Jimmy had "enormous personal needs to be famous".

On to Official Racing

Road racing weekends in California were exuberant and highly competitive affairs usually held on little-used local airports or decommissioned World War II training airfields. On Saturdays, between eight to twelve races were staged, with drivers of small-bore cars or production sports cars competing in defined classes. Those finishing in the top spots would not only be granted a kiss from the local beauty queen and a trophy, but would then compete in one of Sunday's two major races. That was the most coveted prize: the opportunity to race against the 'Big Boys', and maybe display enough talent gradually to become one of them.

All the current aces had followed that path. Phil Hill, for instance, had started in a little MG TC in 1947, and then performed well in a Jaguar XK120. Now 28, he was one of the most successful Ferrari drivers in America. Carroll Shelby had begun racing Jaguars and Allards in Texas, and had now moved to driving top cars in major international events. Ken Miles had first tried his hands in a Frazer Nash back in England, and was now the undisputed American champion of the 'under 1,500 cc' category, driving his own speedy special racer that he had designed and helped build.

When Jimmy arrived at the Palm Springs airfield circuit on Saturday, March 26, he knew the other drivers would not give him any concessions. On the track, neither looks nor acting talent impressed. In that light, his first outing seemed inauspicious. He showed up on the first morning in an open white shirt, black coveralls and leather boots, and carrying a white helmet, cutting a dazzling figure. His white Speedster, with black tonneau cover, seemed more of an aesthetic match than a racer bound for victory. These fashion statements confirmed the race drivers in their opinion that the young actor was there mostly for publicity purposes. They resented this, smirking somewhat obviously when Jimmy and Bill Turnstall, his friend and mechanic for the day, pushed the Porsche, assigned number 23, to the

◄ Jimmy kept keenly abreast of the European racing news, while Dr. Porsche was very adept at using the victories of his cars to promote the marque. This eventually influenced Jimmy when he chose the Speedster. Here at Nice are 'Coupes des Dames' winners of the 1954 Tour de France Automobile: Belgian ace female driver, Gilberte Thirion, and friend, Ingebord Polensky, in a factory-sponsored Gmünd Porsche SL.

starting grid for Saturday's short qualifying race for Class 'F': under 1,500 cc production sports cars.

When the green flag dropped, those perceptions of Jimmy changed rapidly. He boldly shot up from third row to take second place even before the first turn. When the leading cars reappeared completing the first lap, Jimmy was in the lead. After two more laps of the 2.3 mile circuit, he had gained a commanding advantage. Wrote *Motoracing* journalist Gus Vignolle: "His cornering ability with this type of car called for perfect coordination of throttle, brakes and gear shift. By the end of the second lap, he was 400 yards in front. At the end... starter Torres gave him the checkered flag as he roared a good half mile in front of his nearest rival!"

◄ Starting in 1948, the first Porsche cars, the 356 model, were built in Gmünd, Austria. Later the factory moved to Zuffenhausen, near Stuttgart. Gilberte Thirion owned this early model and won several remarkable victories with it, which gained her factory support, as in the Tour de France.

An example of Dr. Porsche's skill in translating impressive victories into enhanced marque image and higher sales. This is the factory's second publicity poster, depicting Porsche's first-ever overall victory in a renowned international event, won in 1952: the grueling 3,211 miles Liège-Rome-Liège Marathon. This is the winning car, driven by Helmut Polensky, husband of Ingebord. ►

PORSCHE

GEWINNT

GESAMTKLASSEMENT
NATIONENWERTUNG
FABRIK-TROPHAE

Lüttich - Rom - Lüttich

5168 km · NONSTOP

◀ Jimmy lovingly cleaning his first real racer, the Porsche 356 Super Speedster in the spring of 1955 next to his house in Sherman Oaks.

Various grainy but precious photos of Jimmy at Palm Springs as they appeared in *Motoracing* magazine, one of America's first sports car racing publications. Gus Vignolle was the publisher, reporter and enthusiast behind it. ▶

The crowd was on its feet. When Vignolle asked Jimmy how he felt at the finish line, he answered: "Gee, I cannot believe it. All I've been doing is racing around Mulholland Drive". With that victory in his first race, Jimmy not only qualified for the next day's big event, he also gained a visible degree of respect, which pleased him immensely.

Now he had time to think about the following day, and the much tougher challenge he faced. The main race would last for one hour, with 27 laps to complete. Some 20 experienced drivers, many with more powerful machines than his, were sure to go all-out for victory.

Jimmy was poised nonetheless, with a well thought-out strategy. Shortly after the start, under a scorching 95 degree sun, he followed a clear-headed plan. He slipped the Speedster into third place behind the two favorites: British ace Ken Miles in his own highly original MG R-2, dubbed the 'Flying Shingle', and Cy Yedor in his own souped-up MG R-1, bought from Ken Miles and further modified.

Jimmy let the stronger duo battle it out while skillfully maintaining his distance and position, behind them. For one hour, the trio led the field unchallenged, battling for car lengths incessantly, but finishing in that order: Miles, Yedor, Dean. This was an extraordinary performance for a total novice driving a new car he had owned for barely four weeks and racing against veteran drivers.

Joe Hyams, his friend and later biographer, wrote: "I remember him pulling into the pits after the race, taking off his helmet, lighting a cigarette and grinning". Ken Miles claimed he had never before seen such latent skill in any driver. "But it was dangerous skill", he added, "the kind that comes as a desperate desire to win". Jimmy saw it differently. He talked about the risk of dying in these terms: "Death cannot be considered

JIMMY DEAN FAR OUT IN FRONT IN DEBUT AT PALM SPRINGS

The Jimmy Dean Racing Story:

LATE ACTOR NATURAL RACE DRIVER, SHOWED TOP PROMISE

JIMMY DEAN FAR OUT IN FRONT IN DEBUT AT PALM SPRINGS

By Gus V. Vignolle

(This is the first article of a series.)

JIMMY DEAN was an unassuming, likeable boy of 24 who was destined to become one of the greatest motion picture actors of all time when his meteoric career was cut short by death Sept. 30.

He died on the way to the hospital after a highway accident that occurred while he was driving to compete in the Salinas road races.

Jimmy was driving a new 550

RACING WAS A RELEASE

Porsche Spyder, a potent German sports car he had dreamed of for a long time.

Only two of the three pictures he made have been released—"East of Eden" and "Rebel Without a Cause." He was an overnight sensation after the first, and his acting ability was acclaimed even more after the second.

His third film, "Giant," is still to be released.

Nearly four months after Jimmy Dean's death, his studio, Warner Brothers, his director and the movie columnists are still being deluged with fan mail.

Louella Parsons, the Los Angeles Examiner and International News Service motion picture editor, recently wrote that a large percentage of her mail urged that Jimmy receive an Academy Award. "They feel," she wrote, "that it would be a shame if he doesn't get some recognition, and I feel the Academy will honor his memory in some special way .."

FILM HIS LIFE

In another column, Miss Parsons pointed out that Jimmy's father, Winton Dean, had been approached by several independent producers about making a film based on Jimmy's life. "I be-

DEAN & STARTER TORRES

love Warners should do this," she wrote. "It would make a great story."

When they get around to making that great story, a vital segment, perforce, must deal with an important phase of Jimmy's life—sports car racing.

The movie angle I know nothing about—except that he was a great actor. Anyway, hundreds of thousands of words have been punched out about his films and his potentialities in that field.

WON FIRST RACE

But I think I know "The Jimmy Dean Racing Story." I knew him personally, meeting him at Palm Springs, where he engaged (and won) in his first race. I covered that race and his two subsequent races at Bakersfield and Santa Barbara for the Los Angeles Examiner. I took the candid photos of him which appear on this page.

Jimmy wasn't exactly the loquacious type, but I did manage to get him to talk about racing at these sports car meets.

Jimmy was a natural driver. He loved cars . . . and he loved speed. It was a release for him

SERIOUS ABOUT SPORT

car," he said matter-of-factly more than once. "I gotta unlimber, let her be right."

NO PASSING FANCY

Many didn't know it, but one of Jimmy's best friends here, Lew Bracker, an insurance man who met him two years ago, will tell you that Dean didn't take cars and racing lightly. Bracker, better than anyone else, knew how dead serious Dean was on the subject. It was no passing fancy.

"His respect for the racing car and the skill required to drive it properly was incredible," Bracker recalls. "This seriousness, his constant study of top drivers and how they took the turns, plus his tremendous competitive spirit, combined to launch him properly on the road to what unquestionably would have been a great racing career.)

WAITING FOR START—A cigaret dangling from his lips, Jimmy Dean, the late actor who showed great promise as a sports car driver, surveys the field at Palm Springs Airport course last spring. He won his first race in a Porsche Speedster.

He said he liked to go . . . go. . . . go. Before a race he'd move away from the pit people, off by himself, drop his head and shake it vigorously as though it were on a swivel. Then he'd paw the ground.

"I've got to loosen up before I get in there and drive that

[The next article will tell of Dean's practice along Mulholland Drive and the actual launching of his brief racing career.]

As a matter of fact, Jimmy got Lew interested in this burgeoning sport. He owns Jimmy's first real racing car, a Porsche Speedster. And today he is a race driver himself. He tooled one of the German cars at the recent Torrey Pines races.

BUYS AN MG

For years—long before he became famous — the late actor wanted to own and race a sports car. In his young mind he pictured himself racing a Maserati through the entire European Grand Prix circuit and in the Mexican road race.

In October of 1954 he purchased a little MG, from which he was to graduate to the Porsche Speedster and then to the powerful Spyder in which his life was snuffed out before he ever had a chance to race it.

ANNOUNCER JIM POLLACK INTERVIEWS DEAN

A SNOW-CONE BEFORE THE RACE

because if you're afraid to die there's no room in your life to make discoveries".

Lew Bracker, his insurance agent, a close friend who later himself became a racecar driver, confirmed: "His respect for the racing car and the skill to drive it properly was incredible. This seriousness, his constant study of top drivers and how they took the turns, plus his tremendous competitive spirit, combined to launch him properly on the road to what unquestionably would have been a great racing career".

Chapter Five

Hollywood Star

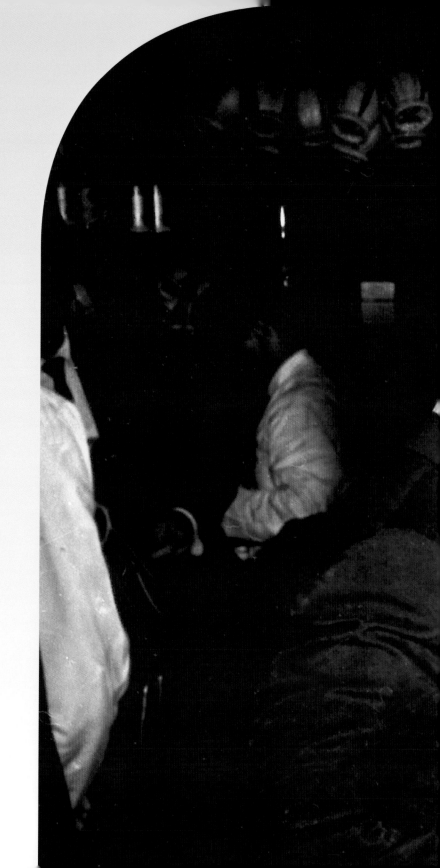

The day after that Palm Springs race, *Rebel* began production and *East of Eden* was distributed to more theatres. Two weeks later it was the biggest box office hit in America. The fan mail and requests for autographed pictures turned into a flood reaching 1,200 pieces a day. The press now even mobbed his friends for interviews. Hollywood's newest star was glowing brighter. Nonetheless, as the production of *Rebel* proceeded in and around Burbank, Jimmy devoted himself to his movie career and to his racing passion during his time off. He practiced driving intensely and tested his mettle in two more official weekend events.

◀ Pages 52-53: By the late summer of 1955, Jimmy had become a genuine star thanks to the smashing success of *East of Eden*. Here he is seen with Sammy Davis Jr. and a very young Ursula Andress, who had just arrived in Hollywood.

▲ Santa Barbara, Memorial Day weekend event, 1955. Jimmy's Super Speedster is on its transporter, bearing an assigned racing number 33.

▲ Labor Day Santa Barbara weekend event, 1955. Porfirio Rubirosa in his Ferrari Mondial. Ambassador at large for the Dominican Republic, Rubirosa was the quintessential international playboy-stud, though also an excellent driver.

Accompanying Porfirio Rubirosa on Labor Day, was a young and vibrant Zsa Zsa Gabor enjoying the racing. ▶

◀ Santa Barbara, Memorial Day weekend event, 1955. Jimmy's Super Speedster in full racing garb, including headlight covers to protect against gravel. Jimmy was always a stickler for style and details.

▲ A very rare photo of Jimmy racing at Bakersfield's Minter Field airport, chasing an American Special. The scattered hay bales show how the rain-soaked track caused many drivers to lose control of their cars.

Dreaming of a faster future. Jimmy looks longingly at the new wonder from Stuttgart: the Porsche 550 Spyder. This one belonged to John Porter. Soon Jimmy would have to have one. ▶

During his practice runs, Jimmy was often accompanied by Bill Hickman. He was the stunt expert on the set of *Rebel,* with great expertise at controlling automobiles precisely through the most unlikely maneuvers. He helped Jimmy rehearse the movie's famous race-to-the-death between two cars and after that, they became fast friends out of their common passion. Hickman, 35, soon spent a lot of time teaching

Jimmy racing techniques: how to power slide through a corner maintaining maximum speed; how to recover from a spin, or how late to brake before a corner to shave nanoseconds off a lap time.

On Saturday, April 30, Jimmy was on the starting grid at Minter Field airport, just north of Bakersfield in Kern County. The weather was foul, with high winds and nasty showers, making the track risky. Turn 3 was

particularly tricky, as the course at that spot ran on turf between two runways for a few slippery hundred yards. This time, Jimmy's qualifying race mixed classes 'F' and 'G', grouping production and modified cars, some with engines up to 1500 cc. Jimmy's assigned racing number now was 123, another number with 3 in the mix. His main adversaries would be Marion Playan in his MG Special, Dr. Bill Eschrich in his Offy Special, and Jean-

▲ Santa Barbara, Memorial Day weekend event, 1955. Checking Ferraris, too, Jimmy here sits at the wheel of the Ferrari Mondial of Josie von Neumann, daughter of the importer and an excellent racer herself.

▶ The Southern California scene produced some exceptional driving talent. Seen here, left to right are Dan Gurney, John von Neumann, Phil Hill and Skip Hudson. Gurney and Hill would go on to Europe and factory Grand Prix teams. Hill would become the first American driver to win the World Formula 1 Championship, in 1961.

Pierre Kunstle, the Swiss resident from Carmel driving a very fast little Devin Panhard boosted by a supercharged engine. Other competitive cars would be OSCAs and Triumph TR2s. Clearly, Jimmy would have his hands full at Minter Field.

When the green flag was dropped, Marion Playan in his MG Special immediately took the lead, with Eschrich in hot pursuit. Struggling on the dangerously drenched track, Jimmy managed to stay within striking distance of

Santa Barbara, Memorial Day weekend event, 1955. Another splendid example of an American Special: Pete Lovely's 'Pooper', or Porsche-powered Cooper chassis and bodywork. ▶

Strolling in the paddock area in his black overalls, cigarette typically jutting from his mouth, Jimmy is in his element. ▼

the leaders, as Kunstle, flogging his fast Panhard, was moving quickly up the field from his ninth position on the grid. On the fourth of six laps, Eschrich took turn 10 too wide and hit the rain-laden hay bales. He managed to recover, but found himself way back. Marion Playan was now holding a commanding lead, while Kunstle and Dean struggled for second place. The supercharged Panhard finally prevailed over the stock Porsche, making Kunstle second and Jimmy third.

This gave the young actor another class win (production cars under 1,500 cc), logging a third outstanding performance, especially in view of the road conditions. The risks had been high. Later that day,

◄ Bakersfield's Minter Field airport event, April 30 1955. In another very rare shot, Jimmy is seen walking back to his Speedster, parked right behind a 1904 Benz racer.

Jimmy in his Speedster arriving at Santa Barbara's airport for the Memorial Day weekend event. The damage from hitting hay bales in his previous race is quite visible. This would turn out to be Jimmy's last race. ▶

The Devin Panhard of Jean-Pierre Kunstle was a typical American Special, also known as a 'mongrel'. Based on the French Panhard chassis, its 750 cc engine was supercharged and its Bill Devin-designed body made of light fiberglass. ▼

Austin Healey driver Jack Drummond slid at turn 3; his British racer hit the soggy hay bales hard, flipped over and crushed the driver. Critically wounded, Drummond died on his way to the hospital.

For his big race on Sunday (cars under 1,500 cc, modified and stock), Jimmy knew that, besides the two cars that had prevailed over him in his own qualifying race, he would face his most serious competition yet. John von Neumann would drive a Porsche 550 Spyder, the latest car from Stuttgart, a pure racer, and the only one yet racing in America. As the California importer for

Porsche, von Neumann had some privileges... Experienced racer Pete Lovely would drive another potent machine, a VW chassis powered by a modified Porsche engine. There would also be two fast Offy Specials (Bill Eschrich and George Beavis), a modified Porsche 356 with souped-up engine (Bill Thomas) and a home-built special with an OSCA engine (Skip Swartley).

This time, the limitations of his car took Jimmy out of the limelight. The weather had also turned hot and dry, eliminating any handicap the heavier cars might have had on a wet track. The 30-lap race started with a

fierce battle for the lead between von Neumann and Lovely in their respective German machines, followed at a distance by an aggressive pack of seven cars in the modified class. Jimmy was left to duel it out with the other production sportsters in mid-field. Lovely held the lead over von Neumann until a broken pin disabled his steering, taking him out of the race. The Austrian and his agile 550 Spyder then won easily, followed by the Offy of George Beavis, Bell's OSCA, Playan's MG Special, then Eschrich's Offy. Kunstle was next in his Devin Panhard, and Swartley finished behind him, closing the ranking of the modified cars.

Jimmy ended the weekend with a strong feeling of frustration. Even the consolation of winning class 'F' was not his. On their last lap, driver Springer Jones in his own Speedster attacked him and the two battled it out around the whole course. Jones finally caught the checkered flag a nose ahead of Jimmy, who was classified 9th. It was time for reflection. In just two weekends of races, he felt he had already pushed the Super Speedster to its limits. He had acquitted himself well, but however much talent he might have, the stock Speedster clearly did not stand a chance against the modified cars; and even less against this amazing Porsche 550 Spyder of von Neumann.

The following four weeks were busy ones for Jimmy as he completed his scenes in *Rebel* and took part in a number of activities connected with the pre-production of *Giant*. All this time, he looked forward to the Memorial Day weekend, which featured CSCC races in Santa Barbara. Despite the frustrations he had experienced at Bakersfield, he would be on the track in his Speedster; he simply planned to drive more aggressively to make up for its limitations. His Saturday qualifying race should provide him with another chance to score a win. As at Palm Springs, he would compete against 'F' class cars only, with no modified racers on the track to spoil his day.

Jimmy, however, did not arrive on the circuit until Saturday night. As racing historians Michael Lynch and William Edgar recently discovered, Jimmy was forced to miss the Saturday race as Warner Brothers instructed him on Friday to stand ready for a make-up test in Burbank Saturday morning. At the track early on Sunday, he soon learned he would have to work harder for the laurels he coveted: the random drawing for the 'under 1,500 cc' consolation race placed him 18th on the grid, clearly a severe handicap in a race of merely six laps, or just 13 miles. His Porsche had been assigned number 33. Unlike star drivers, Jimmy still could not pick his own racing number and 'own' it for the long run. The digit '3' oddly reappeared.

When the waving green flag released the roaring racers, Jimmy was fully determined to win. Weaving boldly through traffic, he moved up to fourth position within five laps. Shortly after that, the car in front of him swerved out of line going into a corner. Forced to choose between hitting that car or the hay bales; Jimmy went for the bales, spun, lost a few places, then recovered. Struggling to catch up, he was soon back in fourth place, still with a slim chance for winning. Pushing harder yet, his senses suddenly registered a loud, sinister clang coming from the engine compartment, immediately followed by a rapid drop in horsepower. One of his four pistons, stressed to the breaking point, had just given up the ghost.

Jimmy could not even finish the race. In his eagerness to overcome his starting handicap, he had taxed his motor beyond its limits. Bill Eschrich won the event in his Offy Special. Ken Miles won the final for under 1,500 cc cars in his 'Flying Shingle', while Ernie McAfee took the laurels in the 'big-bore' event, driving a new Ferrari 750 Monza.

A dramatic scene from *Rebel*. Goon (Dennis Hopper), Judy (Natalie Wood) and Jim (James Dean) look down the cliff in horror at the crashed car on the beach below. An omen for Jimmy's fate? ▶

Chapter Six

Giant
In The Making

◀ Pages 64-65: The lasso as a new tool to master. Jimmy loved to acquire every new skill he could, and he spent a lot of time at Marfa learning the art of lassoing. Obviously, he became quite good at it.

◀ One of the early Porsche 550 Spyders racing in America, identifiable by their extended rear fenders. This is John von Neumann, the California importer, at Pebble Beach in 1954.

Rolf Wütherich, right, smiling here with Porsche 550 ace driver Jack McAfee. A prized von Neumann mechanic, Wütherich would be hired by James Dean, and ride with him on the way to Salinas. ▶

His early racing successes now in the past, Jimmy felt deeply frustrated. The Speedster might have seemed a big jump from the MG, but after Santa Barbara he came to two realizations: first, he needed a much faster car and, second, he could handle such a machine. He had his Porsche 356 towed back to Competition Motors, where he entrusted it for the necessary repairs to Rolf Wütherich, a bright, young Porsche-trained German mechanic employed by Competition Motors. Then 28-years-old and a Porsche employee since 1950, the dark-haired German barely spoke English but held an outstanding reputation for tuning the complex engines from Stuttgart. Jimmy asked Wütherich to save the battered piston.

Then he went to see von Neumann. Expressing his frustration at not having a car capable of challenging for the overall win in the big race, he told the Austrian how

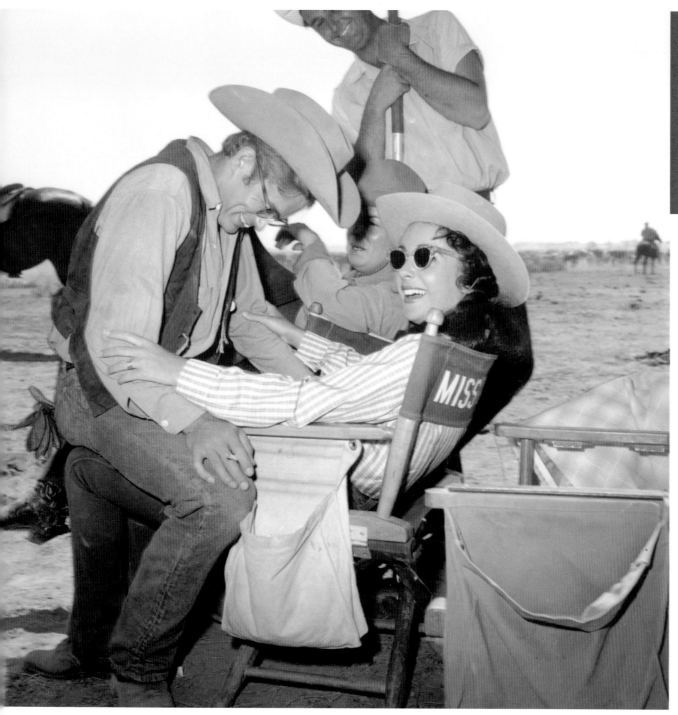

Elizabeth Taylor and Jimmy breaking the boredom of waiting between scenes by 'playing horsies' together. Taylor was terribly affected by Jimmy's death.

Elizabeth Taylor and Jimmy rehearsing a scene from *Giant*. The professional and emotional connection between the two stars is obvious. ▶

impressed he had been by the commanding performance of the importer's 550 Spyder. Knowing a good customer when he saw one, the wily von Neumann explained to Jimmy that the Porsche factory had promised him the first five Spyders destined for American clients right after Labor Day. These would be improved 1955 models, whereas his own was a pre-production 1954 version. The new model would deliver more power; feature a slightly improved suspension, bigger front brakes and refined aerodynamics. He would gladly reserve one of these precious few racers for his now famous friend and racetrack rival.

Jimmy figured he could live with the three-month wait. Though the production of *Rebel*, his second movie, was now behind him, his scenes in *Giant* were to begin within a week, first down in Texas, then back at the

Warner studios in Burbank. This would all take about three months. Warner Brothers had wisely enjoined its newest star from any racing activity during filming of the big $5 million movie - an enormous budget by the standards of the day.

Jimmy's reputation for fearsome driving had grown to such an extent that the movie's director, George Stevens, had forbidden the young star from bringing his Speedster to Texas. He would have to rent a Chevrolet. So, until his role in front of the cameras was duly completed about mid-September, Jimmy actually would have very little opportunity for fast driving, and none whatsoever for racing in sanctioned events. He could not take advantage of a new racecar until September anyway.

He thus accepted von Neumann's offer and picked up the Speedster's mangled piston from Wütherich. After having it mounted on a board, Jimmy later offered it to his father Winton as a trophy. The mangled piston may have been an unconscious symbol of his conflicted feelings towards his father, a loving but distant parent who stood in stark contrast to how he recalled his mother as warm, close, involved and ultra-attentive.

Just before leaving for Texas to rejoin the crew of *Giant*, Jimmy had second thoughts about waiting for the Spyder. Could he really wait that long before getting a racer capable of winning the big events? What if the production of *Giant* was cut short for some reason? What if the Porsche factory delayed delivery of the Spyders to Competition Motors? Delays were more the rule than the exception with European manufacturers of racing cars. Jimmy decided to call on Ken Miles for advice. He was always up-to-date with the racing news from Europe. In fact, he had raced an MG at Le Mans in June and was in the process of negotiating with Lotus to become their California importer.

◀ The oil field of Marfa, Texas, locale of great stretches of the movie *Giant*, Jimmy's third and last film. Here he smokes a cigarette and relaxes during a shooting break.

A classic scene from *Giant*, where James Dean, the aging tycoon, confronts Rock Hudson, the traditional rancher. Of all the main characters in a movie that spans two decades, Jimmy was the only one who looks and acts markedly older - shaved temples and all - while the others only have gray hair. ▶

Not a Porsche! In this scene, Jimmy returns Elizabeth Taylor to the ranch in his old jalopy, the only car he could afford in the movie plot before he struck oil. By the end of the story, Jimmy would be driving a Rolls-Royce. ▶

Lotus was a relatively new but successful manufacturer of 1.1 and 1.5 liter racing cars from Hornsey, England. Lotus founder Colin Chapman placed enormous emphasis on lightweight construction and refined aerodynamics. His cars had an edge in these two important areas and often competed with Porsche for victory on European circuits. Chapman's latest model was the Mark 10, but still only powered by a 1,100 cc engine. That new Lotus might just be a weapon to win even against the Porsche Spyder in America if powered by a bigger American motor, such as an Offy. Jimmy thought so and hedged his bets by placing a firm order with Ken Miles, backed by a deposit. Soon, the factory in England began building the custom order – without an engine. Over the summer, though, Ken Miles was unable to secure the financing for his import venture. It eventually failed and thus the order was cancelled.

Chapter Seven

Silver Bullet
The Porsche 550 Spyder

Silver Bullet: The Porsche 550 Spyder

The Porsche 'Model 550' was launched by the small Stuttgart carmaker in 1953. It was Porsche's second production model and the company's first all-out attempt at making a name for itself in racing. After the early commercial and racing success of the 356 model, the Porsche company had gradually been drawn into a full-fledged racing effort that led to the introduction of 'Model 550/1500 RS', where 1500 stood for the engine displacement and RS for the German *Rennsport*, or sports racer. Founder Dr. Ferdinand Porsche who had died in 1951, would have been thrilled: he had built his flourishing pre-war career by designing highly successful performance cars such as the SSK for Daimler-Benz and the revolutionary V-16 Grand Prix racers for Auto-Union. A mere eight years after the end of World War II, Porsche could now build, sell and field its own racing cars.

When it came time to export the 'Model 550' to the United States, East Coast importer Max Hoffmann gave Dr. Ferry Porsche, son and heir of the founder, the idea to change its technical-sounding German name, and call the racer 'Spyder' instead, with the goal of increasing its appeal to private customers. The new name sounded snappy, and it was a modification of the Italian word *spider* in use since the 1930s to describe open two-seater racing cars. Dr. Porsche wisely accepted Hoffmann's suggestion, and the new designation was eventually scripted in golden chrome on all 550s. The car's remarkable technical qualities, helped by that inspired marketing trick, rapidly turned the new model into a second major success for Porsche both in Europe and America.

Key to the Spyder's racetrack success was its newly designed air-cooled flat-four engine, designated 'Type 547'. Thanks to its highly ingenious design, it could produce 110 hp at 7,800 rpm from a mere 1,498 cubic centimeters. The crankshaft drove the four camshafts and distributors via bevel gears and shafts. In contrast, the contemporary Chevrolet six cylinder called 'Blue Flame' needed a displacement of 3,850 cubic centimeters (235 cubic inches) to deliver 115 hp at a maximum 4,800 rpm. The Porsche design was of course much more complex than the Chevrolet's, featuring twin camshafts on each cylinder bank, twin plug ignition, twin Solex carburetors, dry sump and a double-sided radial cooling fan. Accordingly, the valve-gear alone, for example, required over 20 hours to overhaul. Hence the importance of having a Porsche-trained mechanic, such as Wütherich, on hand during race weekends.

When mated to its new chassis and sleek lightweight aluminum body, the sophisticated powerplant allowed the Spyder to reach 130 miles per hour, a remarkable speed for such a small-engined car. Its curb weight helped, at a mere 1,400 pounds. The tubular ladder chassis and clever suspension design endowed the Spyder - if you had the skill to control its natural tendency to oversteer - with great agility in corners; almost enough, but not quite, to compensate for its power handicap against much bigger-engined cars. A striking indication of the progress between the original Speedster and the new Spyder was the difference between their straight-line acceleration figures.

◀ Pages 72-73: Belgian female ace driver Gilberte Thirion in Ecurie Nationale Belge's new Porsche 550 Spyder. This is the La Roche Hillclimb in March, 1956. Gilberte won, beating renowned champions such as Olivier Gendebien in a Ferrari 250 GT and Paul Frère in a Mercedes-Benz 300 SL. The Spyder proved a winner for years in countless racing venues.

A picture of Dr. Ferdinand Porsche in Gmünd, Austria, standing next to the first Porsche ever built. Nearly sixty years later, Porsche cars remain highly successful both on the sales charts and the race track. ▶

Silver Bullet: The Porsche 550 Spyder

Jack McAfee in John Edgar's Porsche 550 Spyder at Paramount Ranch, 1956. The 1,500 cc Spyder continued to earn outright victories and class wins for years and helped many drivers move up to the higher echelons of racing. Jimmy had instinctively picked the right horse early.

Paramount Ranch Races in California, 1956. Two Porsche 550 Spyders and a 356 Speedster are on the front row. ▶

While it took the Speedster 12.5 seconds to reach 60 miles per hour from a standing start, it took the Spyder a mere 7.2 seconds to achieve the same feat.

Sports Cars Illustrated, in a piece by Griff Borgeson, predicted success as soon as they took their first test: "The savage, lunging character of the car under full throttle is unforgettable. Up to about 5,000 rpm, it feels like one of the thrustiest machines you've ever driven, but then the cams hit their stride and the power *really*

comes on. It felt strong enough to make other 1,500 cc machines seem feeble by comparison". They were right. The Spyder immediately topped the hierarchy of the under 1,500 cc class.

In 1955, only the most powerful cars such as the 4.4 liter Ferraris, or 3.5 liter Jaguars, and 3.0 liter Aston Martins, could outrace the new Porsche; and not always easily. In Europe the previous summer, the 550 racers of the factory team had performed brilliantly in major

races and won the German Sportscar Championship. They had prevailed over much more powerful cars in a number of short distance events. They could not score an outright win in the major endurance races such as Italy's Mille Miglia or Great Britain's Tourist Trophy; their lack of raw horsepower proving too much of a handicap on long distances.

Chapter Eight

The Femme Fatale Beckons

◄ Pages 78-79: Le Mans 24 Hours, June 1955. Three Porsche 550s are shown here vying for the laurels. The first one is the factory car driven by Helmut Polensky and von Frankenberg, which finished 4th overall. The second one is a private Swiss contender, which retired. The third one, driven by the Gloeckler-Juhan pair, finished 6th overall. Such extraordinary results against more powerful cars made the 550 Spyder that much more appealing for racing enthusiasts in Europe and America.

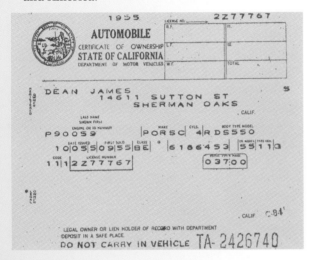

▲ The official State of California Certificate of Ownership for Jimmy's Porsche 550 showing his official address in Sherman Oaks.

▶ The Porsche 550 being prepped for its first race at Competition Motors shop in Los Angeles. On the left are Jimmy and Rolf Wütherich; on the right is Lew Bracker, Jimmy's good friend and insurance agent.

Page 81: Santa Barbara race weekend, Labor Day 1955. Jimmy enjoys the California sun, the paddock and the thrilling atmosphere of sports car racing. ▶

The cast of *Giant* was brought back from Texas to Burbank in July. Toward the end of August, as the film's production neared completion, Jimmy began to look forward to the end of the studio's restriction on his racing. During the Labor Day weekend, he attended the next round of races in Santa Barbara. He was there only as a fan, to see his friend Lew Bracker make his competition debut. It was a difficult two days for Jimmy. It pained him not to be able to measure himself on the track; it hurt him to hear Ken Miles confirm that the new Lotus Mk. 10 he had ordered would not be crossing the ocean anytime soon. It troubled him to see the British driver win again on

Sunday in his ultra-fast, highly modified MG R-2.

Less than two weeks later, on September 16, Jimmy heard at dinner that the updated Spyders had arrived from Germany and that one was even on display in the Competition Motors showroom. Later that night, he felt compelled to drive by Sunset Boulevard and make the right turn on Vine Street. He pulled into the parking lot at 1219 North Vine, got out of his car and looked into the bright room behind the large window. There she was: tightly clad in smooth, shiny silver but for two red pointed streaks on the upper curve of the rear fenders. She beckoned him. Her sensual face seemed to beg for action. Her wheel arches seemed to

demand movement. Her red leather cockpit seemed
to want him. Now, he needed her.

The next night, after filming his last scene in *Giant*,
he attended a private gala premiere of *Rebel* in
Westwood, flanked by a very young and gorgeous
Ursula Andress. Still, The Spyder was foremost on his
mind. On the 19th, coached by Wütherich, he took her
for a test drive down Sunset Boulevard. On September
21, he struck his deal with von Neumann and acquired
her. He would trade in his Super Speedster and hand
over a check for $3,000. In exchange, Jimmy would get
title on the Spyder with the red trim, plus the expert
services of Wütherich during any weekend when he
would race officially. The Speedster's trade-in value plus
the check amounted to the equivalent of about $7,000.
This was the most extravagant purchase Jimmy had
ever made. But the deal he had struck was a good one.
The sticker price of the car alone, equipped as his but
without the assistance of Wütherich, topped $7,000.
No doubt that to recoup his profit, von Neumann
counted on some outstanding publicity from this
celebrity customer.

◄ Elizabeth Taylor and Jimmy, both artificially
aged, during a break while filming the 'Last
Supper' scene in *Giant* in Warner Brothers'
Burbank studios.

Jett Rink, the oil tycoon, as played by Jimmy in
Giant. He is now middle-aged, rich and famous,
but also a drunken wreck. Marlon Brando, Jimmy's
first role model, survived way past middle age to
face such conundrums of real life. We'll never know
how Jimmy would have fared. ▶

With this potent racer, chassis number 550.0055, Jimmy felt sure he could earn outright victories in the forthcoming end-of-season races. He would also gain top-level experience on the track. He later planned to buy a big-engined thoroughbred, and fulfill the last part of this dream. His new salary, just negotiated by his agent Jane Deacy from $1,500 per week to $100,000 per year, took care of the money question. He could now choose any car he wanted: perhaps the potent 4.9 liter Ferrari 375 Plus, winner of the 1954 sports car Manufacturers Championship, or the sleek Jaguar D-type, 1955 Le Mans winner; or even a Formula 1 Maserati 250F, the racer with which international champions would be contending for the 1956 Grand Prix World Title. In fact, he had told Gus Vignolle at Santa Barbara that "his greatest ambition was to [own] a 3-liter Maserati for Grand Prix racing in Europe".

Back in July, Jimmy had already visited the garage of Ernie McAfee, the man who was to Italian sports cars what von Neumann was to their Teutonic rivals. The first Ferrari dealer established on the West Coast, financially backed by Union Oil head Bill Doheny, McAfee loved all Italian makes and raced Ferraris himself. The latest models were always available for his wealthy customers, his establishment also being located on Sunset Boulevard. Among his service customers were Dominican diplomat and playboy Porfirio Rubirosa and real estate entrepreneur Tony Parravano. McAfee's store was likely to be one of Jimmy's future hangouts the moment he felt ready for the big racers.

If Jimmy did succeed in making a name for himself as a top-rated racing driver in America, he intended to cross the ocean and challenge the European masters on their home ground. That ultimate part of his racing dreams may have been inspired by the only woman Jimmy ever truly loved. Italian-born Pier Angeli had a refined beauty and sensitivity rare among Hollywood starlets.

◀ Santa Barbara race weekend, Labor Day 1955. Jimmy, still contractually unable to race as the final scenes of *Giant* were still being shot in Burbank, is there to support his friend Lew Bracker in his first race.

▲ Playboy driver Porfirio Rubirosa and his Ferrari Mondial. Rubirosa dated many famous women, including Barbara Hutton, the Woolworth heiress, whom he later married. In 1965, after hitting many night spots in Paris, he slid off a corner in his latest Ferrari at the Bois de Boulogne, hit a tree and died.

The Femme Fatale Beckons

The two had met at the Warner Brothers studios the previous summer and had immediately fallen for each other. But the dark demons inhabiting both souls soon caused loud and frequent fights. Pier's Catholic mother loathed Jimmy and his reputation. As far as she was concerned, he was not far removed from the devil incarnate. She proceeded to push her daughter into the arms of a man much worthier in her own eyes, one both Italian-born and a Catholic.

In November of 1954, shortly after breaking up abruptly with Jimmy, Pier married singer Vic Damone in Hollywood. Both stung and stunned by her sudden rejection, Jimmy somehow continued to think he could reclaim here. Perhaps he imagined that one feat might make that happen. If one day he could take an Italian Formula 1 racecar and win against all of his British, French or German adversaries, all Italy would adore, even worship him. No people on Earth idolized great racecar drivers more than the Italians, and Formula 1 was tops. Its champions are heroes all over Europe and Latin America. Her mother neutralized, Pier might return to Jimmy.

On the evening of September 21, Jimmy was driven to Villa Capri, a hang-out for rising Hollywood talent, and still his favorite restaurant since Pier Angeli had first taken him there. His Porsche Spyder was waiting in the parking lot, wrapped in a clear plastic shield, with twelve red carnations placed artfully in a bunch over the front hood. Jimmy was beside himself and called on all his friends at Villa Capri to behold his new beauty. Shortly thereafter, he spotted Alec Guinness inside the restaurant. Immediately, he got up and talked the British actor into going outside to look at his Porsche.

Once outside, Jimmy bragged to Guinness about his car's technical highlights and its incredible top speed. The whole scene, including the car's smallish, low look, put the Briton ill at ease, as he painfully remembered in his 1986 autobiography *Blessing in Disguise*. "Please",

◀ Jett Rink, as played by Jimmy, in a scene of *Giant* at the time he is about to become rich. The movie's plot, mimicking Jimmy's life, will appropriately end with a scene called the 'Last Supper'.

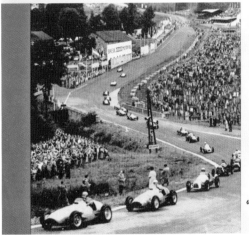

▲ The start of the Formula 1 Grand Prix of Belgium in 1952 at the famous Spa-Francorchamps circuit. Alberto Ascari would win in a Ferrari 500, followed by another Ferrari driven by Farina, a Gordini and a Cooper-Bristol. This is the top racing arena where Jimmy dreamed one day to compete.

James Dean and the love of his life, gorgeous Italian actress Pier Angeli. Because of Pier's Catholic mother, the relationship was doomed from the beginning and both lives ended tragically. After marrying and divorcing Vic Damone, Pier Angeli eventually died of a barbiturate overdose. ▶

he said, "never get in it.... If you get in that car you will be found dead in it by this time next week". That drew a good laugh from the young man from Indiana, who then returned inside for dinner.

Since Jimmy had completed his final scene in *Giant* four days earlier, he was free to race again! Having just acquired a most potent weapon to really show the world his winning talent, he felt elated. He took possession of the car on Friday the 23rd, and started breaking it in cautiously around Sunset Boulevard. His infatuation for the Porsche was instantaneous. Soon, he was on his way to the Warner Brothers studios, where he found George Stevens and most of

the film's crew already hard at work on the preliminary editing of *Giant*.

Jimmy walked to the stern director and asked that he interrupt his activity to go for a spin around the studio's streets in 'his new baby'. To everyone else's surprise, George Stevens proved a good sport and joined him. The low-slung Porsche looked like a futuristic toy car, especially in that setting of warehouse-like buildings. Flashing a wide grin once the director sat on board and the rest of the crew looked on, Jimmy gunned the engine, engaged first gear, then raced down the straight street in a raucous haul. At the end, he spun the car around 180 degrees and roared back to his starting point.

◀ The three great stars of the movie *Giant*, from left to right; were Elizabeth Taylor, Rock Hudson and James Dean. Though by far the junior partner, Jimmy shone the brightest in George Stevens' long saga, which was finally released on October 10, 1956.

A typical Warner Brothers poster for the movie *Giant*. Though the name James Dean appears third after Elizabeth Taylor and Rock Hudson his likeness is alone in the visual, a telling proof of his drawing power. ▶

Stevens got out looking fine, but one of the studio guards did not enjoy the show. Walking angrily towards Jimmy, he warned Warner Brothers' newest star: "You can never drive this car on the lot again; you're going to kill a carpenter or an actor or something".

At about the same time, Jimmy agreed to film a thirty-second spot for the National Highway Committee to promote safe driving. In that commercial, the interviewer, Gig Young, starts by asking Jimmy the fastest he'd ever driven - "about 100 mph or so",

and whether he'd been in a formal race - "I showed pretty good at Palm Springs. ... People say racing is dangerous, but I'd rather take my chances on the track any day than on the highway". Young's final question, before Jimmy, dressed in his cowboy outfit, ambled off the set, was whether he had special advice for young drivers. Per the script, the answer was supposed to be: "Drive safely, because the life you save may be your own." Incredibly, Jimmy uttered: "Drive safely, because the life you save may be *mine*".

Jimmy was terribly impatient to race his new Porsche. However, he would have to wait another week: the next Cal Club race was not scheduled until October 1st, in Salinas. While biding his time, he would take care of the Spyder's final preparations and a few other matters. On Monday the 26th, he took the car to Kustom Kar, a renowned customizing shop in Compton owned by George Barris. He had his assigned racing number, '130', painted in black on the hood and doors of the body.

While this was being done, he impulsively asked Barris also to script the words 'Little Bastard' on the rear cowling, under the black and yellow California license plate marked 2Z77767. The ultimate individualist, Jimmy was basking in one of the many little rays of freedom that brighten everyday life in America, but still even today are rarely allowed in continental Europe. 'Little Bastard' was the nickname Bob Hinkle, his voice coach for gaining a Texas drawl in *Giant*, had given him. In turn, Jimmy called his much taller friend 'Big Bastard'. The scripted nickname on the rear of Dean's Porsche was his facetious note of appreciation to Bob Hinkle.

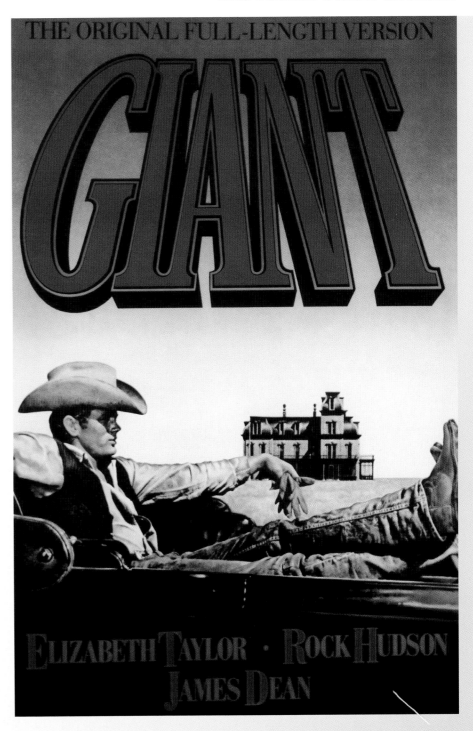

Chapter Nine

On To Salinas
Reaching For Eden

◀ Pages 90-91: Burbank, early afternoon of Friday September 30, 1955. Jimmy is aboard his Porsche, ready to drive north and go racing.

◀ The last fill-up at the outskirts of L.A. before the five-hour trip to Salinas. Everything looks bright, shiny and full of hope. Behind is Jimmy's Ford station wagon pulling the trailer. On the road, Bill Hickman was the driver, and Sandy Roth sat next to him shooting photos.

Lance Reventlow admires a beauty pageant winner as he leans on the racer of fellow driver Carroll Shelby. The son of Barbara Hutton and once called the 'world's richest baby', Reventlow was one of the last three men to talk to Jimmy before the fatal crash. ▶

It was now slightly past 3 p.m. that Friday afternoon, September 30, 1955. Jimmy was steering his Porsche Spyder down the last descent into Central Valley, heading for Bakersfield. He drew deeply on his cigarette and asked Wütherich to check the oil temperature one more time. The German obliged and confirmed a normal reading. Following the Porsche a few car lengths behind was a white Ford Country station wagon pulling an empty flatbed trailer. Jimmy had bought both three

weeks earlier as another investment in his racing career. Inside the Ford were two more people involved with Jimmy on this trip. Driving the station wagon was Bill Hickman, while Sandy Roth sat next to him.

A well-known Hollywood photographer assigned to cover James Dean for *Collier's* magazine since June, Roth had chosen the race weekend in Salinas to complete a photo essay on Jimmy. Jimmy had first met the 38-year-old professional and his wife Beulah on the

set of *Giant*. Jimmy knew of Roth's work and the three became fast friends. When the group prepared to leave the importer's parking lot in North Hollywood at mid-day, Roth had already started shooting pictures. One of the first he took was a frontal shot of the Spyder, with Jimmy and Wütherich holding hands high up in the middle as a sign of a forthcoming apogee.

Jimmy had originally intended to ride in the Ford with his friends, with the Porsche tethered on the trailer. He had in fact bought the Ford after exclaiming: "I don't want to drive the Spyder up north, it's too dangerous". However, and against Wütherich's advice, he changed his mind because he had not found the opportunity to tune the new engine perfectly for racing by putting a minimum of 800 miles on it in and around Hollywood before departing for Salinas. A minor fender-bender on Mulholland Drive in mid-week, requiring a brief stay in the body shop, was one of the reasons.

The previous evening, accompanied by Bill Hickman, he had attempted to drive up the Pacific Coast to gain mileage and experience, but thick fog had forced them to turn back just after reaching Santa Barbara. Both men had gone to bed at 3 a.m. and been up at 8 a.m. Jimmy had decided to drive his new mount to Salinas just before leaving Hollywood, the plan being for Wütherich to accompany him and provide some more counsel during the trip. Additional practice in this much more potent racer would definitely improve his chances of winning the race, Jimmy had reasoned. At noon before leaving, and in a rare show of support, Jimmy's father Winton and Uncle Charlie Dean had showed up at Competition Motors, and the three men then had shared a quiet lunch at Farmer's Market on Fairfax Avenue. Fate had provided for a final farewell between father and son.

At about 3:30 p.m., all four members of the Dean party heard the ominous wail of a siren behind them. When the two drivers checked their rearview mirrors, they glanced at a black and white California Highway patrol car catching up with them with lights ablaze.

A quick look at the speedometer told Jimmy he was going at 70 miles per hour. He knew the speed limit was 55. Patrolman Hunter slid his Oldsmobile past the station wagon and motioned the whole train to pull over. Both Jimmy and Bill Hickman obliged.

As the patrolman left his car, he walked to the Porsche, whose height awkwardly reached to about the level of his knees. The two men in the bucket seats almost seemed to be sitting on the road. After checking Jimmy's driver's license, Officer Hunter began writing a speeding ticket, duly recording the name 'James Dean,' then 'Warner Bros. Burbank' as the driver's business address. He had no idea who this young man in white T-shirt and blue jeans was, but he asked about the highly unusual car and Jimmy explained that it was a Porsche on its way to a race.

The officer appeared briefly impressed. He then cited Jimmy for going 65 in a 55 miles per hour zone and gently admonished him to drive more slowly. Walking to the Ford next, he gave Hickman a ticket also. After the patrol car left the scene, the Hollywood foursome checked the time: it was now almost 3:40 p.m. They agreed to drive on another 150 miles to reach Paso Robles near the coast. There, they would share a quick dinner before undertaking the final trek to Salinas, an additional 100 miles further north.

The Spyder was now entering the outskirts of Bakersfield and Jimmy had to slow down. There was no choice but to go right through town and deal with a series of stoplights. The main thoroughfare, Union Street, was actually a wide boulevard lined with palm trees. Groups of pedestrians crowded the sidewalks at several intersections. The low-slung sportster and its

two occupants were drawing a lot of wild stares. Local town folks were used to seeing racing cars pass through their streets, but this one seemed so streamlined, so metallic, so futuristic, it evoked a science-fiction spaceship. As it was the latest meteor from Stuttgart, driven by the brightest new star from Hollywood, on-lookers who were prompted to think about space travel were not far removed from the truth.

By the time Jimmy left the city limits, it was past 4 p.m. A short while later, the Spyder zoomed by the large hangar of Minter Field, a small military airport on the left side of the road. Jimmy remembered his race there in the white Speedster in early May, struggling against stronger cars and watching von Neumann take the laurels in his 550 Spyder. Now it was September and he, James Dean, had the best from Stuttgart, the same racer as the Minter Field winner, but the improved 1955 vintage. He also had a lot more experience, thanks to his time on Mulholland Drive, and more training, thanks to the advice of his good friend Bill Hickman. He had Wütherich with him to tune the car to perfection and assist in the paddock and from the pits.

The German had told him earlier in the day: "Don't try to win! The Spyder is something quite different from the Speedster. ... Drive to get experience", but Jimmy wanted to score his first big win at Salinas. The Salinas valley, birthplace of John Steinbeck, had been the outdoors site for *East of Eden*. Salinas had helped launch his acting career; now his racing ambitions needed a similar boost. In Salinas, luck would surely be on his side again. He had done everything to entice her.

◀ Bruce Kessler, heir to the highly successful Rose Marie Reid swimwear company, was a friend of Lance Reventlow and became his racing partner.

▲ The Mercedes-Benz 300 SL Gullwing owned and raced by Lance Reventlow in 1955. This was the car that attracted Jimmy to his last stop, Blackwell's Corner, between Bakersfield and Paso Robles.

Shortly before five o'clock, Jimmy and Wütherich reached Blackwell's Corner, a bucolic spot right where Route 466 and 33 intersect. Its lone landmark was a quaint little café, offering snacks and two Richfield gas pumps to drive-by travelers. Jimmy stopped when he noticed a rare, black Mercedes-Benz 300 SL Gullwing parked in the shade near the white building.

He instantly knew it was the special aluminum-bodied racer of Lance Reventlow, one of only 19 built. Jimmy was acquainted with Lance and his passenger and best friend Bruce Kessler, having met them along pit lane during his previous races. The three young men began chatting, boasting about the performances of their respective cars.

Tall, handsome Lance was nineteen years old and the only child of Barbara Hutton, heiress of the vast Woolworth fortune. Fathered by her second husband, Count Kurt Heinrich Reventlow of Denmark, he had been dubbed 'the world's richest baby' by the press when he was born in London in 1936. Lance had become interested in car racing through a succession of step fathers - Hutton had five more brief marriages after Count Reventlow, all of whom except Cary Grant had an interest in fast, expensive cars and in racing them.

Husband number four (1947-1951), Prince Igor Troubetzkoy, sparked Lance's interest. In 1949, the Parisian Prince drove Ferraris and Gordinis in a number of races throughout Europe. Husband number five (1953-54) fanned the flames early in 1954. Dominican diplomat, polo player, playboy-stud, Zsa Zsa Gabor friend Porfirio Rubirosa co-drove a powerful works Lancia D 24 roadster at the Twelve Hours of Sebring, in March of that year, finishing an excellent second. Finally Bruce Kessler, Lance's school chum in Phoenix, himself born into wealth and a racing driver at age 16, finished the job of turning him into a racing enthusiast.

Jimmy quickly found out that Lance was also on his way to the race at Salinas. His mount would be the Mercedes coupe, one of the best production sports cars then available, and the newest symbol of Germany's return to automotive prominence. It was a bigger and heavier car than the Porsche, powered by a 3.0 liter (183 cubic inches) engine. Its pure racing version, the Mercedes 300 SLR, was a race away from wrestling the World Endurance Championship from Ferrari at the hands of, among others, Juan-Manuel Fangio and Stirling Moss. Mercedes would finish first and second in three out of six World Endurance Championship races of the 1955 season, a stupendous achievement.

For Jimmy, whose farm boy years in Indiana were still close, this was heady stuff. Nonetheless, as he puffed on a cigarette and downed a Coke, he surely felt on top of the world at that moment. In a 1957 interview for *Modern Screen*, Wütherich confirmed: "I'd never seen Jimmy so happy. He talked and laughed and seemed very at ease". Once at the race track, he would joyfully mix with his peers, feeling much more comfortable among those young daring men intoxicated by racing and who did *not* mind grease stains, rather than amidst the conceited Hollywood crowd. When earlier in the year, he had shirked the touted celebrity preview of *East of Eden*, he had told his stunned agent, Jane Deacy: "I am sorry, I cannot handle that scene".

In Salinas he would have no one to look up to. He would be there with his own world class Porsche Spyder, accompanied by his own German expert mechanic, and would compete in an official race he felt he could win. That race might not be a major one, but Jimmy would drive hard to snatch victory as if it were the most important race in the world. Confirmed Wütherich in 1957: "The only thought on Jimmy's mind was winning that race. There was no doubt about that, that's all he talked about. We were not talking now about Pier Angeli or of Dean's mother or anything else". Jimmy was on his way to fulfilling yet another dream, to breaking through yet another personal boundary: becoming a world-renowned professional racing driver. To that end, every race counted.

During the short stop at Blackwell's Corner, Hickman and Roth had parked the Ford Wagon nearby to join in the conversation. When Hickman heard Jimmy brag about having pushed his speedometer needle past the 125 mile per hour mark, the stunt driver became concerned for his friend. He told him: "Be careful of the cars turning in front of you. The Spyder is hard to see because of the color and it being so low". Jimmy laughed and urged Hickman not to be concerned: "Don't worry, ... I want to keep this car for a long time, a real long time".

Belgian teammates Olivier Gendebien and Gilberte Thirion drove this Mercedes-Benz 300 SL to victory in the Stella Alpina race on August 28, 1955. Mercedes racers won almost every major race in 1955, but suffered the most dramatic crash at Le Mans in June, where more than 90 spectators were killed. The company withdrew from racing for three decades. ▶

Chapter Ten

Sunset Highway

As Jimmy and Wütherich were getting ready to leave and drive on to their chosen dinner destination, the sun was visibly lower over the horizon and the air becoming cooler. Jimmy put his red jacket on, the one from *Rebel*, and which he now considered his good-luck-charm. He shouted: "Nonstop to Paso Robles", and he and Wütherich leaped back into the low cockpit. The driver's seat belt remained unused, while the passenger had no choice: his seat did not offer any. Jimmy was wearing his prescription glasses with clip-on shades attached. His hands were gloved in beige leather racing gauntlets.

He turned the ignition key; in an instant, the powerful little four-cylinder revved satisfyingly in a low growl. Jimmy gunned it a few times before depressing the clutch. The unique, low-frequency boom of the unmuffled air-cooled engine sounded marvelous to both men. Gear one, shift; gear two, shift; gear three, shift; gear four; the Spyder was now back along Route 466, screaming at close to 100 miles per hour. The road was a narrow two-lane strip of uneven asphalt bordered by soft shoulders of wild grass and weathered cattle fences. Soon, the Ford wagon and its occupants were left far behind. Jimmy and Wütherich were not worried.

To both men, the dry, arid landscape now appeared to be in motion, zooming past their narrowing fields of vision. Time and worldly limits seemed to warp around their speeding projectile. The slipstream racing over the windscreen buffeted their heads, increasing their sensation of irrepressible power. Every now and then, they would catch up with a car towing a trailer carrying a sports car also on its way to the race. The Porsche would quickly roar around and pass them. Jimmy sometimes waved at the driver as he had done with Jack Douglas, towing a Jaguar XK120, shortly after driving through Famoso. He felt so great, so relaxed now. The last week had passed so quickly!

◀ Pages 98-99: Famous photographer Sandy Roth, having followed James Dean for 85 days on a special assignment for *Collier's* magazine, takes this driving shot of the Porsche 550 through the Ford's windshield, while passing Bakersfield. Little did Roth know this would be one of the last pictures of Jimmy alive.

◀ Jimmy smiling with pride showing off his racing trophies and helmet. To him, these was much more worthwhile than an Oscar.

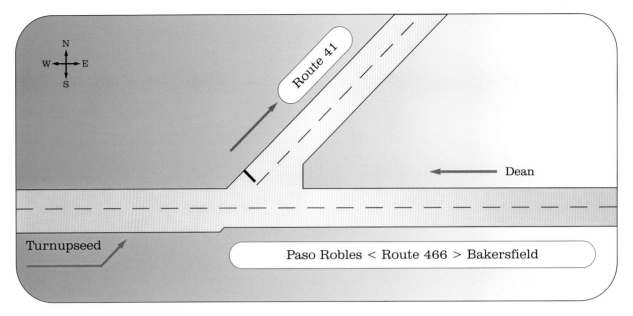

The small Spyder was now more than 20 miles past Blackwell's Corner, approaching the tiny rural town of Cholame in the northeast corner of San Luis Obispo County. Following the directions of Wütherich, Jimmy had continued to open up the engine and thus had increased the distance between them and the station wagon. As they crested a low hill past the twisting turns of Polonio Pass, Route 466 suddenly stretched for a mile and a half in front of the two men in a nearly perfect straight line. The landscape on either side appeared painted in soft red hues by the glowing disk setting directly ahead.

At half the distance to their horizon, on the right side, Route 41 merged with the main road at a narrow angle, as a twig joins a main branch. (see diagram) There were no buildings or trees anywhere to obstruct the view.

The only vertical objects in their field of vision were wooden telephone poles on the left side of the road standing in a row every 120 yards or so, and the thin picket lines of the cattle fences planted about ten feet inside both uneven, grassy shoulders.

At the instant that straight stretch of road appeared before Jimmy and Wütherich, about two miles ahead of the Porsche, a young man by the unlikely name of Donald Turnupseed was driving eastward on Route 466. He was steering a two-door coupe version of the 1950 Ford Custom Deluxe. It was an unusual-looking car, made more so by the two-tone black and white paint job slicing it in half horizontally.

Turnupseed, 23 years old, had just spent three years in the Navy and was now a freshman at the California Polytechnic Institute - known as Cal Poly - in San Luis Obispo, where the G.I. bill was helping him finance this education. He was returning home for the weekend to see his pregnant wife in Tulare, about 150 miles inland from his school.

His general direction was northeast, coming from the west; Jimmy's was northwest, coming from the east. During their respective trips that day, their individual itineraries would share only about 8 miles of the same stretch of road, or a maximum elapsed time of three minutes given their combined speeds. The two itineraries crossed at the intersection now lying between them. Turnupseed planned to make his usual left onto Route 41; whereas Jimmy was aiming directly ahead on a lane straight and clear as far as his eyes could see, but for another westbound car about 500 feet ahead of him. It was backlit by the shimmering orange sun now slowly descending behind a distant set of hills stretching across the horizon.

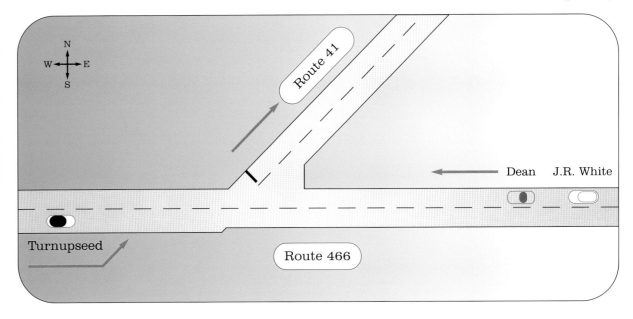

◄ Facing east, the fatal intersection as it later looked. Jimmy's Porsche would have come down directly at the photographer from the straight road. Turnupseed's Ford would have come directly at the photographer's back, then aimed to turn left on the curving side road.

The Custom was Ford's first new postwar design. When the model came out in 1949, its styling was innovative. It was the first American mass production car to have straight-through lines from front to rear, integrating the fenders entirely as part of the body shape. Its grille was a sumptuously chromed affair with a jet's nose cone-and-ring design adorning the middle. With a weight of more than 3,000 pounds, its rail frame chassis was barely adequate. While its front suspension was independent and featured coil springs and wishbones, the rear remained a solid axle guided approximately by two longitudinal leaf springs. As a result, the Ford Custom steered imprecisely and at best gave its driver an uneducated feel for the road. In 1955, even its styling looked dated.

Turnupseed, a straight young man belonging fully in the conventional camp, probably thought his customized Coupe looked racy with its special paint job, rear wheel well covers and white-walled tires. He probably believed the two-door style with a short hard top made it sporty. He sure was proud of the 100 horsepower delivered by its 3.9 liter (239 cubic inches) flathead V-8. But Turnupseed's Ford was no driver's car.

Jimmy was now closing fast on the sedan preceding him, accelerating to overtake it. A Pontiac was coming at him in the eastbound lane, but Jimmy estimated he had just enough speed not to worry about it. As if in a racing maneuver, he swerved into the left lane, rushing past the car he had just been following. His timing was so close, the driver of the oncoming Pontiac took fright and veered to his right, straddling deep into the shoulder. The road was wide enough at 26 feet to allow three cars abreast, but only just. Jimmy swerved away from the left lane back into his a split second ahead of the Pontiac, grinning widely, hair flapping in the wind.

The driver of the car he had just passed, accountant John Robert White of Price Waterhouse, looked in disbelief as the Porsche increased its distance ahead of him. He knew the intersection with Route 41 was just ahead, that fatal accidents had happened there before. As his eyes scanned the road ahead, he noticed the next eastbound car, a black and white vehicle, about a quarter mile ahead. That car seemed to be hesitating. Sensing trouble he told his wife "Watch this".

Before nearing the familiar intersection, Turnupseed had accelerated past 60 mph to overtake a car driven by two young men on their way to a football game in Bakersfield. Now he proceeded to move left toward the median a bit early, without activating his turn signal. He knew the spot; the sun behind him gave him a clear view through his windshield. Ahead on Route 466, he could see only a family sedan coming the other way, still distant enough he could make a safe turn. A second later though, as his left wheels were just about to bite on the dotted divider line, he suddenly caught sight of a low-lying vehicle closing in fast.

Sunset Highway

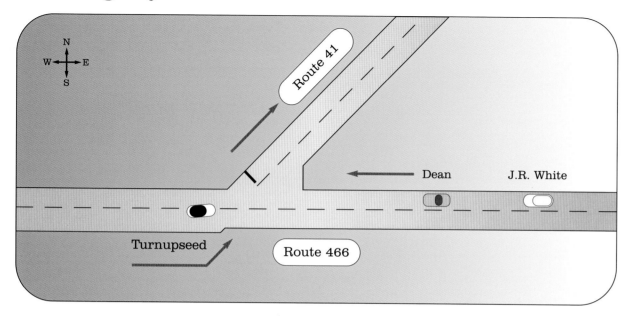

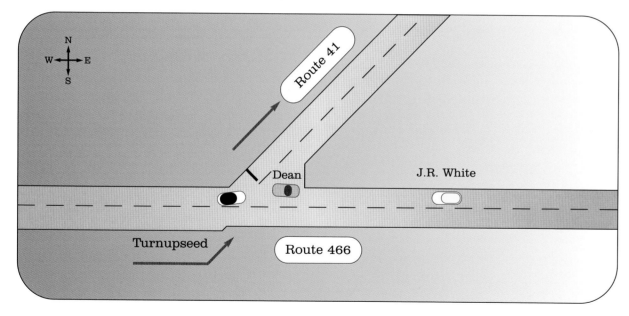

Jimmy now noticed the Ford veering gradually toward the middle of the road. He lifted his right foot instantly and told Wütherich: "That guy up there's gotta stop, he'll see us".

Turnupseed, startled by this apparition, slammed on his brakes reflexively, but his hands remained locked in the left turn position. The tires of the heavy Ford imprinted 39 feet of skid marks on the road, the left tires encroaching gradually into the oncoming lane.

Jimmy was now fully aware of the emergency and figured a solution. The right lane widened to his right at the intersection. That was the only way to give the other driver more time to think. Or was the worst now inevitable?

Turnupseed lifted his foot for a split second, his frightened mind scrambling his judgment, and he kept turning left. The little silver car was growing rapidly in his field of vision.

Jimmy was now operating on pure racing instincts. Braking would make him lose control of his steering. Instead, he veered right a little, giving Turnupseed more room on the left.

Turnupseed now began to hear the growl of the onrushing Porsche. In panic, his right foot gunned the Ford engine. The young Californian was hoping against hope he could safely complete his left turn before the Porsche reached him. Therefore, he was still aiming left.

Jimmy was not seeing the expected relief. The room for maneuver on the right was still getting tighter, not greater. Veering to the right any sharper, he would lose the car. Too late for braking ...

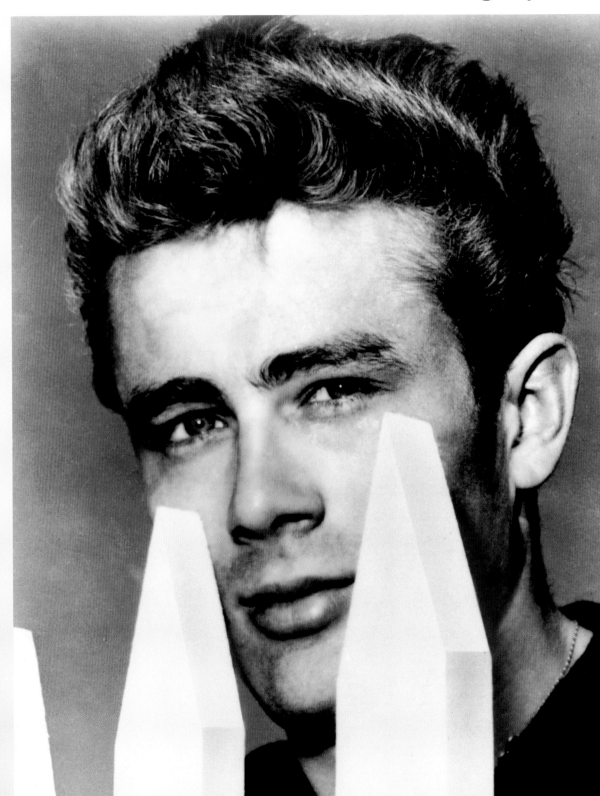

James Dean in *East of Eden*. Are the white spikes a picket fence or the fangs of fate? ▶

Turnupseed saw now he would not make it through. In continued panic, his feet switched pedals again, slamming on the brakes. His arms were still frozen in the same position. Emitting an ugly screech, the Ford's tires left 22 new feet of skid marks on the asphalt, scarring completely across Jimmy's lane.

Jimmy was now way to the right in the middle area of the Y intersection, his last hopes quickly fading. The big black and white slab ahead was running out of time to veer off and leave him just enough space to recover.

Turnupseed sized up the situation at the last moment. His arms freed, he desperately thrust his steering wheel to the right. It was too late. The Porsche's left front was inches from hitting the Ford's own left front fender.

Jimmy reflexively stiffened his entire body, his feet pushing full force against the floor.

Sunset Highway

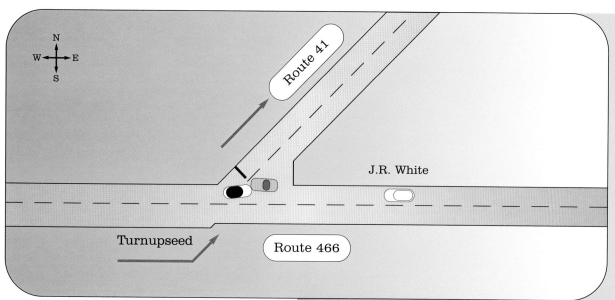

The crash site minutes after the accident. Jimmy's limp body is already in the ambulance. The young man in the black T-shirt is Donald Turnupseed, the Ford driver. Rolf Wütherich, with broken jaw and leg, is still on the grassy side and about to be placed on the gurney. ▶

John Robert White and his wife both saw it. The two mismatched automobiles collided violently in a loud bang and an exploding cloud of debris. The Porsche's left front fender, on the driver's side, impacted the front of the bulky American coupe at an angle, pushing back its engine and breaking the metal block. Turnupseed saw an arm flailing over the Ford's hood in a futile protective gesture.

The sturdy German chassis bent instantly and the left side of the Porsche crumpled. The dashboard was shoved into the cockpit and to the right, bending in the middle. Then the silver projectile took off and cartwheeled. Its hood and rear cowling flew open as Wütherich was flung from his seat.

The Ford spun around clockwise under the impact, while continuing on its eastbound trajectory.

▲ The accident scene, showing the crashed Ford
Custom, the tire marks and the ambulance.

Its front smashed, its left fender discarded, it finally
stopped sideways across what a moment before had
been Jimmy's westbound lane. Turnupseed sat in shock
in his seat, motionless and in pain.

Wütherich landed on the grassy shoulder to the
right, just as the Porsche's remains came to a rest
nearby on its four wheels, only inches from a telephone
pole. Jimmy lay sprawled on his back across the
bucket seats, his foot caught under the crushed pedals.
His head hung strangely backwards over the passenger
door. From his multiple wounds, blood was running
down the red fabric of his windbraker and the red
leather of the trim.

It was 5:45 p.m. Less than thirty seconds had
elapsed since Jimmy had pronounced the words:
"he'll see us".

Dr. Robert Bossert was the physician on duty that
evening at War Memorial Hospital in Paso Robles.
The radio system had alerted him that an ambulance
was rushing towards the hospital with two serious car

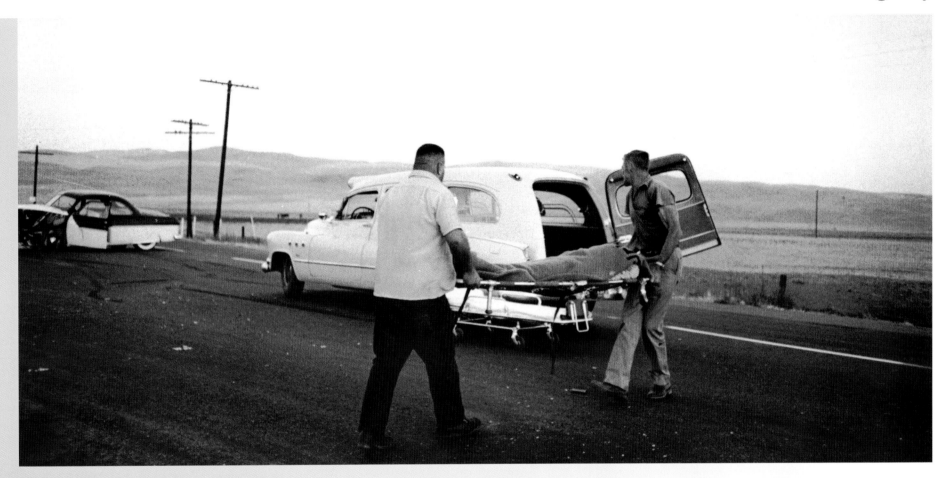

▲ The two medical helpers carry Jimmy's body into the ambulance. For Hollywood's newest star, it is the moment of transition between life on earth and immortality.

crash victims. When he saw the long white Buick speed up the road, warning lights flashing, night had fallen. He noticed that two cars towing trailers followed the Buick. The two ambulance attendants moved Wütherich out of the ambulance and passed the gurney on to waiting medical attendants. They did not remove Jimmy. Instead, they asked Dr. Bossert to look at him first.

By then, six anguished people had gathered from the other two vehicles. From a light beige Ford Wagon towing an empty trailer, Hickman and Roth had emerged and were now looking at the dark interior of the ambulance. They had arrived at the accident's scene minutes after the crash. Hickman had held Jimmy's head in his lap until his friend's pinned foot was freed

from the smashed pedals. They had watched as Jimmy's limp body, then Wütherich's, were loaded into the ambulance.

They had followed the white Buick on its twenty-minute race to the hospital. Right behind them another car had tagged along towing a trailer carrying an intact 1954 Porsche Spyder.

It was von Neumann, who had been on the same route and destination as Jimmy. Accompanying him were *Road & Track* photographer Jerry Chesebrough and their respective wives. The four friends had reached the crash scene a few minutes after Hickman and Roth.

Dr. Bossert had now climbed into the back of the ambulance next to the second gurney. The first thing the physician noticed about the other victim was the strange angle of his neck. It did not bode well. When he gently rotated the head, he heard a muffled grating sound. The neck was broken from the whiplash, the spine shattered. He found many more fractured bones: both forearms, in several places; the ribcage; the left leg; probably also the cranium since the forehead seemed bashed. Bruises and lacerations scarred the entire body. Dr. Bossert turned to the six people looking at him outside of the ambulance. With a stern face, he declared the victim dead on arrival.

In the commotion at the crash scene, Hickman of course had been too upset to notice a supreme irony. He and Jimmy were quite familiar with the Ford Custom. A black two-door Custom convertible was the street car driven by Buzz, Jimmy's rival in *Rebel*. Buzz reveled in driving around town, along with members of his gang, teasing Jimmy. Pitted against a similar car, Jimmy had now lost his own nerve-wracking 'Chickie Run', and his life.

Inside the hospital, Wütherich had also been examined. He proved to be the lucky one. The young German had suffered multiple fractures of the jaw when his face hit the dashboard, then a crushed left femur a split second later. He had not lost consciousness. It would be a long recovery, marked by pain, but he would make it.

Turnupseed was gathering himself following this awful accident. After the debris was cleared, he had given his deposition to the police at the scene, claiming, "I couldn't see him", as if to counter Jimmy's last words. Now he found himself in the company of the last few drivers-by who were preparing to leave the spot. His nose, chest and left shoulder were flashing pain. Other than that, he was all right and could walk normally.

The problem was that his car had been towed away and Tulare was a good 50 miles to the northeast. Nobody, not even the policemen, offered him a ride. All were headed to either Paso Robles or Bakersfield, not to 'nowhere' on Route 41. Turnupseed was left to hitchhike. By the time he was dropped off in Tulare, it was 11 p.m.

▲ This is the Kodak strip, with clear but reversed numbering, from Sandy Roth's last pictures of Jimmy. Some people have speculated that Roth took an image of his face as he lay dying in the car. This film strip disproves that theory.

Another, very symbolic view of the fatal intersection. Bakersfield is the last city through which Jimmy had passed and Paso Robles the town where he and his companions planned to have dinner. At the spot shown here, Jimmy's life ended. ▶

Chapter Eleven

Funeral and Prejudice

Funeral and Prejudice

Jimmy's burial took place eight days later in Fairmount, on Saturday October 8. His family members were all there, along with 3,000 fans and admirers. But only a few faces from Hollywood made the trip to the flat plains of Indiana. Most of his colleagues and co-workers simply sent flowers, as did Warner Brothers. Jimmy was too new a star and not yet world famous. That would come a little later; after the world could see *Rebel* and *Giant* and discover the highlights of the 'Little Bastard's' short and extraordinary life.

Among the numerous wreaths adorning the church in Fairmount were twenty-four white roses sent by Barbara Hutton. Unbeknownst to all, including her son Lance Reventlow, this gesture was in memory of a single passionate night she had had with Jimmy eight months earlier at the Beverly Hills Hotel. That evening had started as a chance encounter at Googie's, a joint popular among young Hollywood stars, and featured a wild ride on Jimmy's Triumph motorbike back to her hotel. Those two lonesome souls, 23 years apart in age, had instantly felt a strange affinity for each other. According to Hutton's notebooks, they made love all night and Jimmy had talked about "the exhilaration of taking chances, the pursuit of the heightened moment, intensity for its own sake".

Little did either know that night that, with the exception of Wütherich, Hutton's son Lance Reventlow would be the last man to talk with Jimmy before he died; that Lance would later show just the sort of spirit Jimmy had exalted in. In July of 1957, he would start a company called Reventlow Automobiles, Inc. (R.A.I.) in Los Angeles. Single-mindedly dedicating it to building an all-American sports car capable of beating the best European racers, he would give it the unusual name Scarab. Lance and Jimmy had shared some fun times together on race tracks and on the Hollywood night scene. The wealthy youth may have chosen that name for his racing cars after hearing Jimmy telling a friend: "If a man can bridge the gap between life and death, if he can live on after he's died, ... to me the only success, the only greatness ... is in immortality". The scarab, indeed, was a sacred animal and the main symbol for immortality in ancient Egypt.

The first two Scarabs, powered by a Chevy V-8, were completed by early August of 1958. They proved splendid racers and met with remarkable success all season. Then Lance aimed much higher too quickly by joining Formula 1, but not achieving the success he had hoped for, he closed R.A.I. in 1962 and left the racing world entirely. Ten years later, at age 36, he was killed in the crash of a private plane near Aspen, Colorado, without fulfilling his undoubted potential. Unlike Jimmy, Reventlow was born into wealth. He never had to scrape, to struggle, to invent himself from the ground up, against all odds. His short fame is long forgotten. The sacred scarab only beamed on Jimmy.

James Byron Dean's funeral service started at 2 p.m. at the Fairmount Friend's Church. Several eulogies were heard. They had a somber, religious tone that Jimmy would surely have loathed. Pastor Xen Harvey was the best. He titled his eulogy 'The Life of James Dean - A Drama in Three Acts'. Calling his death "only the end of Act Two and the beginning of Act Three", he finished by affirming: "The career of James Dean has not ended, it has just begun. And remember, God himself is directing the production".

Jimmy would have liked the pastor's last sentence. But he probably would have preferred the words pronounced later by Bill Hickman: "In those days, racing was what he cared about the most. I had been teaching him how to put a car in four-wheel drift, but he had plenty of skills of his own. If he had lived, he might have become a champion driver". Or he would have chosen the reflections of his friend Lew Bracker, quoted earlier. Bracker himself later became a racing driver because of Jimmy.

Yet, Jimmy's reputation for 'reckless driving' was such when he left for Salinas that the responsibility for the accident was automatically assumed to be his. The fact that several witnesses confirmed seeing him driving 'very fast' shortly before the collision, and the report of his speeding ticket earlier in the day, eliminated any doubts some might have had. The small size of his 'foreign car' and its 'irresponsible purpose,' i.e. racing, made it all that much easier to believe it was 'his fault.' The basic facts of the accident were nonetheless immediately obvious. The day after the collision, the *Mirror News* of Los Angles headlined Jimmy's death on its front page and wrote: "The California Highway Patrol said a car driven by Donald Turnupseed, 23, ... turned left off Highway 466 onto Highway 41 and collided almost head on with Dean's car".

But in an adjacent front page column, the newspaper's Entertainment Editor, Dick Williams, was already spinning the story: "A Warner Brothers Studio executive who used to watch James Dean zoom out of the studio in his fast foreign racing car often shook his head and declared: 'That crazy kid is going to kill himself'. Last night his prophecy came true as one of the most brilliant newcomers I've discovered on the Hollywood scene was killed in his white Porsche in a highway accident near Paso Robles". Williams had the car color wrong, and also misunderstood Jimmy's devotion to racing, his talent for it, and the fact that the accident was not his fault.

◄ Pages 112-113: James Dean, the young actor soon to be famous. Not only was he intense and manic about acquiring the best acting skills, but at 5'10" with blond hair and blue eyes, he was also extraordinarily handsome.

Jimmy on the set of *Giant* in Marfa, Texas, posing for Sandy Roth. Many have said James Dean had a death wish, using this picture and others where he posed in a coffin to argue their point. Indeed, Jimmy was very aware of death, having lost his beloved mother when he was only 9. But he loved life, as this entire book shows. ►

At the inquest in San Luis Obispo in mid-October, a jury quickly declared Turnupseed not guilty of any fault. The questioning of the witnesses, which included Turnupseed himself, took just over two hours. The local Sheriff and the Under Deputy District Attorney asked leading questions automatically assuming that the young Hollywood actor had died for only two reasons: his foreign car was small and vulnerable - 'without a top' - and he was driving recklessly fast. Local boy Turnupseed, son of a respected local businessman, youthfully responsible and a new father, seemed to have behaved properly all along as he proceeded to make his left turn; he "just didn't see the Porsche".

When the precise sequence of events on Route 466 was finally established following an exacting review one year later, as detailed above, no one picked up the story.

The Warner Brothers poster for *Rebel*, with Jimmy sporting the red windbreaker that would become one of his trademarks.

One of the first newspaper headlines announcing the death of James Dean. The text already presumes his 'reckless driving habits' were to blame. These false impressions are completely debunked in the detailed analysis of the accident in this book. ▶

Jimmy was by now famous around the world; his violent death was part of his legend. It was too late to reverse the first impression created by a superficial interpretation of the tragedy. That impression is predominant around the world to this day.

There were other factors of course favoring the myth of self-immolation. Jimmy was the 'rebel' challenging the establishment of which the press was then part. He was always in the company of new starlets and raced German cars. For a majority of older Americans, he might as well have been Lucifer. His death was coming to him.

Donald Turnupseed had to be the good guy. A Navy veteran with service in Korea, he was driving home to rejoin his pregnant wife. He worked in his father's store.

FILM STAR KILLED IN CRASH

France Orders U.N. Delegation Home

Action Taken After Rebuff Over Algeria

UNITED NATIONS, N.Y., Oct. 1 (UP)—The French delegation to the U.N. Assembly was ordered home today and the permanent French representative in the U.N. planned to follow in 48 hours, a delegation spokesman announced.

He could not make clear on the basis of present information whether the withdrawal would be permanent, he said. The French delegation walked out of the U.N. yesterday after a one-vote margin ordered France's rule over Algeria taken up in Assembly

James Dean Is Victim as Cars Hit Head On

PASO ROBLES, Oct. 1 (AP)—Actor James Dean, the surly, brooding Caleb of the movie "East of Eden," was killed last night in the head-on highway crash of his brand new sports car near here.

The 24-year-old actor, often compared to Marlon Brando, was driving to a road race in Salinas, the location site for the movie which catapulted him to stardom.

Dean, an enthusiastic amateur sports car racer, was the second young Hollywood leading man killed recently. Robert Francis, the "Willie Keith" of "The Caine Mutiny," died July 31 in a plane crash at Burbank.

The California Highway Patrol said a car driven by Donald Turnupseed, 23, of 1001 Academy St., Tulare, turned left off Highway 466 onto Highway 41 and collided almost head-on with Dean's Porsche spyder. Turnupseed, a student at California Polytechnic College at San Luis Obispo, suffered minor in-

MOODY STAR

'Crazy Kid' Death Was Feared

BY DICK WILLIAMS
Mirror-News
Entertainment Editor

A Warner Brothers Studio executive who used to watch James Dean zoom out of the studio in his fast foreign racing car often shook his head and declared:

"That crazy kid is going to kill himself."

He was the ideal young man, the loving husband. He was Abel, or 'Aron' in *East of Eden*, the dutiful son, whose fate was to bring eternal shame to the rebel sibling, the one who had dared challenge their common father, Adam. Naturally then, newspapers and magazines at first were only too happy to turn Jimmy's spectacular death into an integral part of his insurrection, that of a strange new star who shot through the sky then burned, finding a fitful end to a life at the edge, brilliant as it might have been.

To quote the prophet Isaiah (14:12-15):

"How art thou fallen from heaven, O Lucifer, son of the morning! ... For though hast said in thine heart, I will ascend into heaven, I will exalt my throne above the stars of God.... Yet thou shall be brought down to hell, to the sides of the pit".

But soon, the boy from Fairmount would overcome the Biblical judgment.

Chapter Twelve

Instant Immortality

Instant Immortality

By the time *Rebel Without a Cause* was released to movie theaters, four days after Jimmy's death, the cult of James Dean was already turning into a global wild fire. The new movie fanned the flames mightily. Fan clubs were started across the Americas, Europe and even Iran and Japan. Letters from all over the world, addressed to Jimmy, arrived by the bagfull at the Warner Brothers studios daily. Some people were even convinced that James Dean was still alive, but so mutilated that he was slowly healing in a hide-away. Others claimed that though dead, he would one day return 'reincarnated'.

Such were the passions triggered by a young man who thus became the world's first teenage idol. Elvis Presley, still merely a regional star and one year away from reaching national fame, said in a televised interview: "I want to be like James Dean". He had watched *Rebel* a dozen times and knew some of the dialogue by heart. Elvis would become in many ways a bigger star, but without benefiting from the merits of one of Jimmy's favorite quotes: "Live fast, die young and have a good-looking corpse". James Dean was the bright super nova that heralded the beginning of the youth revolution, a phenomenon that would shake the establishment to its core within a decade.

David Dalton, author of the best biography of James Dean, titled *The Mutant King* posits that part of the phenomenon was made possible by America's post-World War II fast-increasing affluence. Insidiously, by 1955, that affluence had spread for the first time ever to a large, relatively homogeneous group: adolescents. But until *East of Eden*, they had no heroes with whom to identify. Wrote Dalton: "The idols of their parents were lifeless symbols of the status quo. James Dean gave adolescents a face, *his* face, and with this communal image they could define and defend themselves.... James Dean... cut adolescents loose from the family and gave them a weapon to effect change: childhood armed".

◀ Pages 118-119: A Sandy Roth photo that could be captioned 'James Dean looking at us from the heavens'.

◀ Jett Rink, as played by Jimmy in *Giant*, has just struck oil in his tiny patch of land. In an instant, his life changes and he is about to become very rich. This is an unintentional but remarkable metaphor for Jimmy's life, when he was cast as Cal Trask for *East of Eden* in 1954, moved to Hollywood and soon became famous.

Jimmy and a mannequin in an art studio, in a superb Sandy Roth photo, displaying the actor's emotion and deep need for affection. ▶

American childhood in the late 1950's was indeed armed with money, and it gradually would deploy this weapon to redefine a newly molting America by means of a revolutionary culture. Rock 'n Roll, jeans, mini skirts, pot, hippies and other novelties, all the way to young Ralph Nader versus General Motors and the anti-war movement, were on the way. These developing social phenomena were able to catch and spread widely because the dam was breached in 1955 by a mythic figure whose brief, brilliant vault across the heavens gave his iconic face to the global transformation to come.

In early 1964, when Bob Dylan released his epochal
album *The Times, They Are A-Changing*, he symbolically
seized the lead from the previous generation by
proclaiming its impotence. The rebels were now fully
in charge:

Come mothers and fathers,
Throughout the land
And don't criticize
What you cannot understand.
Your sons and your daughters
Are beyond your command
Your road is rapidly agin.'
Please get out of the new one
If you can't lend your hand
For the times they are a-changin'.

James Dean was the first 'God of Youth' or, as it
was phrased then, 'Teenage Idol'. Many since have
succeeded him, but he is the one who opened up the
gates of a new aspirational 'Eden'. Though his life story
was ever so brief, he earned a rightful immortal place in
our modern pantheon.

◀ James Dean, regular guy, here petting a Siamese cat. For all his antics and manipulations, Jimmy was still a farm boy at heart.

Jimmy looks to the heavens, perhaps wishing he could fly like his companion. ▶

◀ The monument at Cholame, site of the accident, designed and financed by Mr. Seita Ohnishi.

JAMES DEAN
1931Feb8 — 1955Sep30pm5:59 ∞

The Monument at Cholame

The monument seen in the picture here was commissioned and built by Mr. Seita Ohnishi, Japan's greatest James Dean fan. Living in Kobe, Mr. Ohnishi is an influential businessman who as a teenager was deeply touched by James Dean's movies and mythology. Japan has a very large Dean fan club to this day. As an adult, Mr. Ohnishi became a dedicated collector of James Dean memorabilia, including the Sandford Roth photo collection, many examples of which are featured in this book.

The monument, situated very near the accident site, commemorates Jimmy's life and death, ending with the symbol for infinity, signifying immortality.

The Porsche and the Ford,
fateful instruments of
death and immortality,
in a Cholame garage the
day after the fatal crash. ▶

Whatever Happened to Jimmy's Porsche Spyder?

After the crash, Jimmy's 550 Spyder was parked in a garage in Cholame. After the early commotion died down, the engine and transmission were sold to Dr. Bill Eschrich who fitted them into a Lotus. Later, the Porsche body was banged back into some shape and rented by the Greater Los Angeles Safety Council as an exhibit designed to promote safe driving among young people. Eventually, the carcass was shipped by train to Florida. During that trip it mysteriously disappeared, never to be found again.

Acknowledgments

This book was a work of love and many people helped me turn it into a reality. First, there were my two children, Alexandre and Olivia, who inspired me to produce this book. They are very creative and I wanted them to be proud of their Dad as an author.

Then there is the trio of Jim Sitz, Michael Lynch and William Edgar, all from California, racing historian extraordinaires and most wonderful gentlemen who provided encouragement, photos and technical details of the first order. Next is Bob Devlin, who researched James Dean many years ago and provided vital documents, information and insights. Most important, Mr. Seita Ohnishi of Japan, and his lawyer in San Francisco, Mr. Yuji Mitani, were extremely cooperative and provided priceless photos in the most agreeable way.

Then there is Ken Vose, best friend and renowned automotive writer; he provided support and an unique perspective all along. My friend Jacques Mertens from Brussels, Belgium comes next. A successful entrepreneur, he is also a Porsche fan and provided photos no one else has that make this book even more special. Finally, my publisher Glyn Morris and his wife Jean, were good-humored, extremely helpful, patient and cooperative from beginning to end.

It's been a great adventure and the end product makes me really proud.

Philippe Defechereux

Book Title	Author	Year
James Dean		
Blessing in Disguise	Alec Guinness	1985
Boulevard of Broken Dreams	Paul Alexander	1994
James Dean	Marceau Devillers	1985
James Dean - A Portrait	Roy Schatt	1982
James Dean - American Icon	David Dalton	1984
James Dean - Behind The Scenes	L. Adams/K. Burns	1990
James Dean, Little Boy Lost	Joe Hyams	1992
James Dean Revisited	Dennis Stock	1987
James Dean - Shooting Star	Barney Hoskyns	1989
James Dean - The Memory of the Last 85 Days	Sandy Roth/Seita Ohnishi	1987
Poor Little Rich Girl - Barbara Hutton	C. David Heyman	1983
The Death of James Dean	Warren N. Beath	1986
The Fifties	David Halberstam	1993
The Mutant King	David Dalton	1974
The Unabridged James Dean	Randall Riese	1989
Related Automobiles		
American Road Race Specials	Allan Girder	1990
Classic Porsche Racing Cars	Michael Cotton	1988
Lotus - The Sports Racing Cars	Anthony Pritchard	1987
Motoracing	Gus V. Vignolle	1956
On a Clear Day, You Can See General Motors	John De Lorean	1979
Porsche - Excellence Was Expected	Karl Ludvigsen	2003
Porsche 356 & 550 - A Pictorial History	Henry Rasmussen	1992
Porsche 356 & RS Spyders	Gordon Maltby	1991
Power Behind The Wheel	Walter J. Boyne	1988
Scarab - Race Log of the All-American Specials	Preston Lerner	1991
The American Automobile - A Centenary	G. N. Georgano	1992
The Concise Dictionary of Motorsport	George Bishop	1979
The Encyclopedia of Motorsport	G. N. Georgano	1971
Vintage Motorsports	Issues Nr. 5 and 6	1992

Photograph Credits

Index

Design	Ben Gibbs - Motion Design
Printer	Star Standard Industries Pte Ltd., Singapore
Printing	Four color litho on Roland Speedmaster
Page size	300mm. x 230mm.
Text paper	170 gsm Stora Enso Matt Art
End papers	140 gsm Woodfree
Dust jacket	135 gsm Glossy Art
Inks	Toyochem
Body text	9/13pt Univers 45 Light